What people are saying about
Practical Virtue

I have known Randy Hain for more than fifteen years and have long appreciated his passion for helping the next generation of leaders thrive in the workplace. His newest book, *Practical Virtue*, is a much needed and timeless resource for all early career professionals and aspiring leaders who wish to acquire critical leadership soft skills, grow personally, and become leaders who are worth following. I believe this is not only a critical resource for these future leaders to absorb and practice, but also a practical tool more senior leaders should utilize to create guided conversations with their younger colleagues at work. I strongly recommend *Practical Virtue*, and I am excited to endorse this amazing book!

—**Tim Elmore**, Founder of Growing Leaders and www.TimElmore.com, and author of *A New Kind of Diversity*

Randy Hain's *Practical Virtue* captures his unique insight gleaned from his work with executives and leaders across a broad spectrum of organizations. This book will aid the aspiring and early career professional alike as they seek to efficiently and effectively transition into the modern workforce. Practical Virtue provides a guidebook and a roadmap for early career success that will create tomorrow's ethical leaders.

—**Chad Carson, PhD**, Dean of the Brock School of Business at Samford University

Practical Virtue is an insightful guide for aspiring leaders looking to build a foundation of character-driven leadership. As a Division I athlete, team captain, and coach, I have seen firsthand how virtues like accountability, discipline, and humility are critical to success—both on and off the field. Randy Hain masterfully presents these virtues not just as ideals but as practical skills that can elevate leadership and career growth. His actionable insights make this book a must-read for any young professional striving to become a servant leader worth following.

—**Liz Harrison**, Masters of Marketing student at University of Florida, Division 1 Athlete, and future business leader

Practical Virtue provides guidance into living a life grounded in integrity and purpose. Randy Hain offers advice on how to apply timeless virtues to everyday challenges, helping readers build stronger character and more meaningful relationships. It's an invaluable resource for anyone, especially early career professionals, committed to personal growth and leading with intention. I strongly recommend this book!

—**Misty Brown**, Associate Commissioner for the Southeastern Conference

For early career individuals looking to build a strong foundation in personal and professional growth, Randy Hain has written an indispensable guide. With wisdom from eleven acclaimed books, Randy delivers actionable insights on accountability, candor, relationship building, and more, all tailored to help young professionals thrive. This timeless resource will empower the next generation to navigate their careers with confidence and integrity.

—**Camye Mackey**, EVP and Chief People, Diversity & Inclusion Officer for the Atlanta Hawks

Randy Hain has had a profound impact on my leadership journey, from my time in collegiate athletics to my post-graduate career, and I have consistently admired his commitment to helping individuals reach their full leadership potential. His latest book, *Practical Virtue*, is an essential resource for anyone, especially early-career professionals seeking to develop leadership skills grounded in authenticity. Randy's insights are invaluable for both young professionals looking to build a strong foundation and seasoned leaders mentoring the next generation. I highly recommend *Practical Virtue*—it is a powerful tool for anyone striving for personal and professional growth.

—**Kathryn Cosgrove**, Director of Global Enterprise Accounts for UPS

Randy Hain has once again compiled a helpful book that should be in the hands of every young professional. Filled with practical, everyday strategies that are often lost in the hustle and bustle of growing your career, he brings the reader back down to earth . . . to the bare essentials of what it means to be a good person at work instead of just an employee. This will be a book that will be on my desk to in the years to come to refer to as I grow into leadership roles.

—**Bain McCullough**, Account Executive, AJC Freight Solutions and early career professional

Young professionals starting out face challenges, no doubt. Navigating the early stages of a career can feel overwhelming, but the ability to connect with a network of seasoned professionals who open doors, offer practical advice, and genuinely invest in your success is an invaluable gift. It's a gift you should absolutely accept and open. Randy Hain's *Practical Virtue* is like having that network in book form. It's packed with actionable advice that empowers you to drive your own success forward. I'd hire anyone who embodies even half the virtues Randy explores. They are the qualities that make a true leader—no matter your age, someone worth following. This isn't just a good read; it's a practical toolkit for building a fulfilling and impactful career and a crucial resource for anyone serious about taking charge of their professional development. Enjoy the journey!

—**Lisa Bigazzi Tilt**, CEO of Full Tilt Consulting

Randy Hain's *Practical Virtue* is yet another secret revealed for those looking to get ahead in their careers while seeking balance in their personal lives. Randy has spent decades coaching some of the most successful senior executives in business, all while writing numerous bestselling books, in an effort to help them manage the trials and tribulations that come with large responsibility. In *Practical Virtue*, he shares the most helpful of these critical virtues and truths with those just beginning their careers. Randy's perspective is a gift that I wish a lot of us had as we began our career journeys many years ago.

—**Eric Simpson**, VP of National Distribution for AT&T

Randy Hain's *Practical Virtue* is an invaluable resource for early-career professionals seeking to build both character and leadership skills. With real-world insights and actionable advice, this book bridges the gap between personal growth and professional success, making virtues tangible and practical for aspiring leaders. Randy Hain's approachable style and wealth of experience make *Practical Virtue* a must-read for those who want to lead with integrity and purpose. Candor and kindness, joy and hard work, clarity and authenticity—all virtues each person could benefit getting a little better at—thank you, Randy, for another great read!

—**Kate McCombs, PhD**, Assistant Professor of Leadership at Samford University's Brock School of Business

Practical Virtue by my friend Randy Hain is an insightful guide for emerging leaders, offering actionable advice on cultivating essential virtues like Acceptance, Authenticity, and Generosity. Drawing on real-life examples from his experience as an executive coach, Randy demonstrates how these virtues can enhance leadership, build trust, and promote growth. This book presents virtues not as abstract concepts but as practical soft skills vital for success in any leadership role. Whether you're a student, early-career professional, or seasoned leader, *Practical Virtue* offers valuable lessons to help you grow personally and professionally.

—**David McAnally, Jr.**, VP, Learning and Development/Partner, LocumTenens.com

Practical Virtue is a must-read for anyone looking to develop the core virtues that drive personal and professional success. While it's valuable for readers at any stage of their career, it's especially the book I wish I had read earlier in my own journey. Written by a deeply authentic expert on virtues, it offers an A-to-Z guide covering everything from Acceptance to Vulnerability—key traits that shape strong leaders. What I love about it is how easily you can refer back to topics whenever needed. Whether you're unsure where to begin or need help tying the pieces together to become a more effective leader, *Practical Virtue* is the resource you need.

—**Kevin Webb**, CFO Iconex Paper

I recently had the pleasure of reading *Practical Virtue* by Randy Hain, and I must say, it was a truly enlightening and inspiring read. As someone who is passionate about investing in the next generation of leaders, this book resonated with me on a deep level. Randy's emphasis on the importance of consistently practicing virtue in both our personal and professional lives is a message that is much needed in today's world. By choosing to act in accordance with positive character traits such as gratitude, generosity, kindness, justice, humility, and patience, we not only become better leaders but better human beings as well.

For me, what sets this book apart is Randy's approach to presenting virtues as essential and critical skills for leaders to embrace fully. Each chapter is filled with real-life stories, actionable best practices, and insights that are not only valuable for personal growth but also for developing leadership skills that others will be eager to follow. As in previous writings, I appreciate Randy's humility in acknowledging that there is no magic formula for success, but rather, it is through consistent practice and application of the virtues discussed in the book that we can accelerate our personal and professional growth.

I highly recommend *Practical Virtue* to anyone who is looking to enhance their leadership skills, experience personal growth, and cultivate virtuous habits that will not only benefit them in the workplace but in all areas of life. This book is truly a bridge to a better life and career, and I believe it has the power to inspire and empower readers to reach their full potential. I applaud Randy for creating such a valuable resource, and I am excited to see the impact it will have on the next generation of leaders. Thank you for sharing your wisdom and insights with us.

—**Juan Perez**, Chief Information Officer at Salesforce

In *Practical Virtue*, Randy Hain provides those who seek to be successful business leaders an essential resource for promoting both individual and organization excellence. He has drawn on his many years of coaching and mentoring to identify the key character traits practiced by the most successful business leaders. Everyone knows that ongoing professional development in relevant knowledge, human talents, and skills is a necessary ingredient for success. But Randy points out that leaders who are most worth following are consistently those who also develop and practice the moral virtues in the workplace. Aspiring young leaders, and even experienced executives, will benefit from the practical and actionable lessons contained in this book. *Practical Virtue* will help you attain your goals.

—**Mike Bickerstaff,** Founder and President of Virtue@Work

Have you ever noticed how some people are consistently living with a hope in life that others, and maybe yourself, don't seem to grasp? The word that comes to mind is flourishing. They seem to be flourishing even when things are not always going their way. They have something ingrained in them that allows them to lead a life of acceptance, authenticity, gratitude, and joy—traits we all wish would come to us naturally. Randy Hain's *Practical Virtue* points the way to a flourishing life personally and professionally. These time-proven virtues have been around for several millennia, and Randy has done a magnificent job of modernizing, personalizing, and making them practical. This is a fantastic book to share with others whether you are a mentor or looking to be mentored. Buy this book and after you read it, take the risk of sharing it with those you care about and start a conversation around each virtue. You will never regret it!

—**Ray V. Padrón,** Retired CEO, Brightworth Private Wealth

In my thirty years of teaching college business students, Randy Hain stands out as our most impactful and frequently invited guest speaker. His ability to translate timeless virtues into practical leadership skills has made his work essential reading in our Sports Industry Program at Samford University and the Brock School of Business. *Practical Virtue* masterfully distills his wisdom into an essential guidebook for emerging leaders, seamlessly integrating character development with professional growth. For anyone aspiring to become a leader worth following, this book gets my highest recommendation.

—**Darin White, PhD**, Margaret Gage Bush Distinguished Professor, Executive Director, Sports Industry Program and Center for Sports Analytics at Samford University

This book is a must-read for college and early career professionals. Randy Hain shares timeless wisdom that can help anyone in their career journey. It is especially useful for young people who are committed to growing personally and professionally. The book is a wonderful resource for those who strive to exhibit strong leadership traits and make ethical and virtuous decisions both at work and in their daily lives. Each chapter offers sound counsel and provides opportunities to learn and reflect. As a young professional and a recent graduate, I'd highly recommend this book to others.

—**Sylvie Wages**, Communications Coordinator for Emory University Marketing and Communications

Practical Virtue is a book I would recommend to leaders of all ages. However, it will especially benefit early-career team members as they prepare for greater leadership roles. In his characteristically thoughtful style, Randy Hain provides clear links between the soft skills needed for success in the workplace and essential virtues. This connection elevates the importance of cultivating virtue at work. His stories also provide actionable ideas to impact the workplace culture, regardless of role.

—**Corrie Michals**, Marketing Executive and Coach, NaviGateway Services

Randy Hain brings wisdom and insights into his new book, *Practical Virtue*, and it is a must-read for anyone who is looking to lead a better life and have a more fulfilling career. Randy has been a friend and mentor for almost twenty years, and his books and advice are treasured gifts to his audiences.

—**Jo Ann Herold**, Vice President, Marketing & PR at Georgia State University and author of *Living on a Smile*

Randy Hain has done it again! Except this time, his timeless concepts are geared toward college seniors and young professionals. I am encouraged and inspired by *Practical Virtue* applying to our next generation of marketplace, civic, and nonprofit leaders. Randy captures the essence of impact by offering time-honored virtues through this guidebook for young and aspiring leaders around the world. I wish I had known all this wisdom when I was starting out in the marketplace! This book is carefully curated to inspire courage, confidence, authenticity, and many other necessary yet often forgotten behaviors needed in the world today. Here's to our next generation of leaders who will learn valuable life lessons from this master teacher!

—**Ash Merchant**, President of Lionheart Partners

Randy Hain's guidance has been invaluable in helping me recognize the untapped potential I had beyond the football field. Through his insights, I've learned how to translate the discipline, resilience, and teamwork from my Division I football career into dominating the workforce. His new book on emerging leaders is sure to inspire countless professionals, just as he has inspired me. I have no doubt it will be a game-changer for those looking to maximize their impact and have successful careers.

—**Joshua Mathiasen**, Zimmer Biomet sales representative, former Division One Athlete

Randy Hain's *Practical Virtue* is an essential guide for early-career professionals looking to develop strong leadership skills through the lens of timeless virtues. Drawing from his extensive experience as a mentor, executive coach, and author, Hain seamlessly connects soft skills with fundamental character traits such as integrity, humility, and accountability. While *Practical Virtue* is particularly valuable for young professionals, its wisdom applies to leaders at all levels. It's a resource that encourages self-reflection, promotes ethical decision-making, and ultimately helps individuals become leaders worth following. Highly recommended for those eager to build a career rooted in authenticity and purpose.

What sets this book apart is its blend of real-life examples, actionable insights, and thoughtful storytelling, making abstract virtues practical for the modern workplace. Whether discussing the power of gratitude, the necessity of candor, or the importance of resilience, Hain provides an invaluable roadmap to help professionals flourish on their career journey. With Randy as your guide, you will cultivate habits that lead to both career success and personal fulfillment.

—**Grant Means**, Author, *Financial Foundations & The Peachy Pig* series and President, Start Now

In *Practical Virtue*, Randy Hain is able to distill a lifetime of his own work into critical lessons for early-career professionals. Through a combination of stories, specific examples of lessons learned, and actionable best practices, Randy is able to effectively illustrate how to incorporate the various virtues into both personal and professional life. Having worked with hundreds of young professionals and as a longtime board member for the Bryan School of Business at The University of North Carolina and Greensboro, I have seen firsthand the critical need aspiring leaders have for the active development of soft skills. *Practical Virtue* provides a much-needed framework for early-stage leaders to begin their lifelong development journey and provides a method for the reader to become a better leader almost immediately.

—**Gary Fly**, Founder of PerformanceCXO

PRACTICAL VIRTUE

An Actionable Guide to Help You Become a Leader Worth Following

Randy Hain

Author of *Becoming a More Thoughtful Leader*

Foreword by Dr. Paul J. Voss

President of Ethikos and co-author of *Merchant Saint*

SERVIAM PRESS

Copyright © 2025 Randy Hain

All rights reserved. With the exception of short excerpts used in articles and critical review, no part of this work may be reproduced, transmitted or stored in any form whatsoever, printed or electronic, without the prior written permission of the publisher.

ISBN: 978-1-7377244-9-0 (softcover)
ISBN: 979-8-9891099-0-6 (e-book)

Published by Serviam Press, LLC
www.serviampress.com

This book is dedicated to the next generation of leaders.

You inspire me and give me great hope for the future.

CONTENTS

Foreword by Dr. Paul Voss xix
Introduction 1
CHAPTER 1   **Acceptance** *Practicing Acceptance and Seeing Burdens as Blessings* . 5
CHAPTER 2   **Accountability** *Taking Ownership and Accelerating Your Career* ... 11
CHAPTER 3   **Authenticity** *Let's Be Real* 17
CHAPTER 4   **Candor** *A Roadmap to Candid Work Conversations* 25
CHAPTER 5   **Civility** *Fostering Greater Civility* 35
CHAPTER 6   **Clarity** *Getting Clarity Right* 41
CHAPTER 7   **Commitment** *Facing Veracruz Moments* 47
CHAPTER 8   **Contentment** *What Is Success?* 53
CHAPTER 9   **Credibility** *Credibility Matters* 59
CHAPTER 10 **Curiosity** *Cultivating the Curiosity Skill Set* 67
CHAPTER 11 **Generosity** *Thoughtfully Considering the Power of Generosity* .. 77
CHAPTER 12 **Gratitude** *Live Life Gratefully* 81
CHAPTER 13 **Hard Work** *What It Takes to Make the Most of Opportunity* 85
CHAPTER 14 **Humility** *A Man I Know* 91
CHAPTER 15 **Joy** *The Attractiveness of Joy* 95
CHAPTER 16 **Kindness** *The Importance of RAPKG* 99
CHAPTER 17 **Learning** *The Journey from Learning Jobs to Doing Work We Love* .. 107
CHAPTER 18 **Mentorship** *Mentoring the Next Generation* 113
CHAPTER 19 **Morality** *The Need for a Moral Compass* 119
CHAPTER 20 **Patience** *Six Best Practices for Being More Patient with Others* 127
CHAPTER 21 **Reflection** *Don't Be Afraid to Be Countercultural* 133
CHAPTER 22 **Relationship Building** *Essential Lessons
            for Better Business Relationships* 137
CHAPTER 23 **Self-Discipline** *The Power of Self-Discipline and Intentionality* . 145
CHAPTER 24 **Service** *The Regular Heroes among Us* 151
CHAPTER 25 **Simplicity** *Embracing Simplicity* 157
CHAPTER 26 **Stewardship** *The Abundance Mindset Activates Stewardship* .. 165
CHAPTER 27 **Thankfulness** *Making the Most of a Once Treasured Practice* .. 173
CHAPTER 28 **Thoughtfulness** *Five Traits of a Thoughtful Leader* 181
CHAPTER 29 **Vulnerability** *Turning Our Vulnerabilities
            into Something Positive* 187
Conclusion 193
Additional Resources 197
Acknowledgments 199
About the Author 201

FOREWORD

We do not use the word *magnanimity* much today, but it carries a deep, almost noble resonance in the context of human virtues. It refers to the quality of being generously forgiving, especially when faced with adversities, insults, or challenges. At its core, magnanimity involves a noble spirit—one that rises above petty grievances, seeking to act with great-heartedness, open-mindedness, and unselfishness. In the context of Randy Hain's work in this book, magnanimity can serve as an underlying theme, offering both a philosophical lens through which we examine the human experience and a practical guide for interacting with the world around us.

The term itself comes from the Latin *magnanimus*, meaning "great-souled." It implies not just a rarefied kindness or generosity but an elevation of the self beyond narrow, self-centered concerns. Thus, to be magnanimous is to act in ways that reflect a larger vision of the just and worthy, particularly when we are in managerial or executive positions. Magnanimous people do not lower themselves to the level of retaliation but instead strive to rise above, embodying the virtues of patience, wisdom, and grace.

Both Aristotle and St. Thomas Aquinas wrote extensively about magnanimity, each offering insights into its significance. Aristotle, in his *Nicomachean Ethics*, considers magnanimity to be the crowning virtue, a balance between excessive pride and undue humility. For Aristotle, magnanimous people know their worth and act in accordance with that knowledge, seeking honor rightly but not out of vanity. St. Thomas Aquinas, drawing from Aristotle, integrates this virtue into a Christian framework, emphasizing that true magnanimity aligns with divine grace. Aquinas suggests that a magnanimous person seeks to achieve great things not for personal glory, but in service to God's greater good, making this virtue a reflection of both human and spiritual excellence. In both thinkers, magnanimity stands as a virtuous ideal, a mark of nobility that transcends mere self-interest.

Magnanimity is an essential counterbalance in a world where pettiness, bitterness, and ego can often dominate. To embody this virtue means to reject the smallness of the ego in favor of a broader, more compassionate perspective. It invites us to understand others' flaws and limitations with a sense of empathy and even kindness, recognizing that we, too, are imperfect. It's not about blind forgiveness, nor is it an excuse for passivity in the face of injustice. Rather, magnanimity requires the courage to transcend immediate impulses in favor of something more enduring—a better way of being that uplifts both the individual and the collective.

In relationships, whether personal or professional, magnanimity holds the potential to heal wounds that might otherwise be irreparable. It calls upon us to set aside grudges, embrace generosity of spirit, and offer others the opportunity to rise alongside us. It is, in other words, our highest and best selves—the "Better Angels of Our Nature," as eloquently put

FOREWORD

by Abraham Lincoln. This quality does not diminish the need for accountability or fairness; instead, it amplifies our capacity for understanding and reconciliation. In a society increasingly defined by division and misunderstanding, magnanimity offers a beacon of hope—reminding us that greatness of soul can often turn conflicts into opportunities for growth and connection.

Randy Hain's exploration of virtue invites readers to reflect on the meaning and application of magnanimity. It challenges us to consider how often we allow ourselves to be dragged down by the smallness of conflict and how much we could elevate our interactions if we embraced a more magnanimous approach. In a time when it's easy to hold on to grievances or to seek retribution, magnanimity reminds us of the importance of letting go, of looking beyond the immediate frustration, and of striving for something greater—something that transcends the boundaries of self-interest and touches the universal need for compassion and understanding.

At its heart, magnanimity isn't about perfection or saintliness (for as we know, that's an impossibly high bar indeed). It's about embracing the human capacity for goodness and striving to express it even in the face of adversity. This very infectious quality can inspire others to act with similar generosity and courage, creating a ripple effect that can impact the nature of both individual lives and society as a whole. Through magnanimity, we find a path that leads not only to personal peace but to collective harmony, where the smallest acts of kindness and the grandest gestures of forgiveness combine to create a world more reflective of our shared humanity.

This book is taking you on a journey that will help you

achieve your God-given potential. Read and reflect carefully on the various chapters, implement the best practices, and engage with mentors and friends to discuss what you are learning. The one virtue Randy Hain didn't write about is magnanimity, but the entire book and the lessons it contains, is pointing you toward living this noble virtue.

—Paul J. Voss, PhD, Associate Professor at Georgia State University, co-author of *Merchant Saint*, and President of Ethikos

INTRODUCTION

I have the privilege of speaking with college students, early career professionals, and emerging leaders in the workforce on a regular basis. I also actively coach and mentor one on one a number of early career professionals each year with new faces joining this loose cohort fairly frequently. I am energized by these conversations and have a passion for not only investing in these future leaders but also learning from them.

Recently, I was reflecting on my many conversations with this group and how I can better serve their professional and personal development and help them unlock their potential. I have long believed and consistently shared with others that this group will soon run the world, and I am excited for the future they will create. But I also feel that older generations like mine owe it to this next generation of leaders to share with them our knowledge and experiences, listen to their ideas, and openly discuss mistakes we have made and the lessons learned. We have an obligation to actively guide, coach, and encourage them to be prepared to lead . . . and lead well. My hope is that these emerging generations will embrace the mantle of leadership and become leaders *actually worth following*.

There are so many approaches we can take to help this generation lead well, become better human beings, and do the right thing at work, and I would suggest the most compelling and helpful path leads through sharing and modeling the merits of the consistent practice of virtue. The journey to become a leader worth following must necessarily involve a journey to become a better human being. *This is why virtue matters...*

To consistently practice virtue means to habitually and deliberately act in accordance with moral principles, repeatedly choosing to behave in a way that aligns with positive character traits like gratitude, generosity, kindness, justice, humility, and patience, even in difficult situations. It's essentially making ethical behavior a regular part of the way you live and your decision-making process. Virtues are developed through repeated daily practice, becoming ingrained habits that guide your actions naturally. All of us, regardless of title or experience, have the ability to develop, practice, and refine our virtuous behavior. Hopefully, we learn the merits of virtuous behavior from our parents, our faith, friends, and our community. Even if that is not the case, virtues can always be learned and applied in everyone's life.

As an executive coach and the author of a dozen books, I have long been focused on creating practical tools for my clients and sharing helpful insights with my broader network. Over the last fifteen years, I have written about dozens of helpful virtues in my blog posts and books. The book you are about to read is my humble attempt to pull together favorite virtues from my previous work as well as new writing with

INTRODUCTION

a focus on helping early career professionals become great leaders. In each short chapter, you will encounter true stories from my coaching work, experiences with friends and my own experience, along with actionable best practices to help you better understand and apply each virtue in your life.

Where this book may differ from other books on virtue is that each virtue is presented as a necessary soft skill leaders and aspiring leaders should fully embrace. For example, *patience* is certainly an admirable virtue, but practicing patience is also a great way to live *and* lead. My hope for you is that as you work your way through the short and actionable chapters, you will learn invaluable leadership skills, experience considerable personal growth, and pick up life-changing, virtuous habits that will help you do the right thing at work and become a leader others are eager to follow.

This book on practical virtues is meant to be a bridge to a better life and a better career, but it is *not* the end of the journey. There is no magic formula, but consistently practicing what you learn in this book will greatly accelerate your personal and professional growth. The Resource section at the end of the book will point you to additional books and websites that will help you continue the growth you have hopefully experienced with the help of the work you are about to read. I stand on the shoulders of giants as I offer through *Practical Virtue* a simple introduction into helpful virtues for life and work. I hope what you read here will be the catalyst for further exploration into the writers who have shaped my thinking on virtues over the years: Plato, Aristotle, St. Thomas Aquinas, Josef Pieper, Alexandre Havard, Dr.

Peter Kreeft, Dr. Donald DeMarco, David Brooks, James L. Nolan, Dr. Tim Elmore, Dr. Paul Voss, and most importantly, the teachings of Jesus Christ in the Gospels.

If you are a more experienced leader eager to help and mentor the next generation of leaders, I hope you enjoy the book and will share copies with students, early career professionals, and any aspiring leaders in your sphere of influence. We need to not only pass the leadership baton on to them but also be willing to accompany them in the early stages of their journey. If you are seeking an actionable guide to facilitate meaningful conversations on substantive topics with this group, *Practical Virtue* was mainly written for this purpose.

If you are an early career professional eager to grow into a leader worth following, this book will help you, challenge you, and offer you a glimpse into a compelling future where you will be more engaged in your work, leading with excellence and reaching your God-given potential. I want you to know I am cheering for you and excited to accompany you on the journey.

Thank you, and I wish you the best of luck.

CHAPTER 1

Acceptance

Practicing Acceptance and
Seeing Burdens as Blessings

We often live with this illusion. With the impression that all would go better, we would like the things around us to change, that the circumstances would change. But this is often an error. It is not the exterior circumstances that must change; it is above all our hearts that must change.

Fr. Jacques Philippe, *Searching for and Maintaining Peace*

Many years ago, one Sunday after Mass, one of our parish priests asked me and my wife how he could pray for our family. We asked him to pray, as we frequently did, for our oldest son's future and that he be healed of his autism. He looked at us thoughtfully for a moment and then shared some guidance with us that has been transformational in how my wife and I view every aspect of our lives. He encouraged us to shift from praying for healing and pray instead for *acceptance*.

Let me explain.

He said there was nothing wrong with asking God to heal our son. But we first needed to ask for the ability to fully accept the beautiful gift of our child *exactly as God created him*. By asking for healing first, we were in essence asking God to improve on His creation without first understanding the lessons and blessings His gift has provided our family. We have always viewed our oldest son as a blessing and know we could not possibly love him more than we do now. But we may have mistaken love for acceptance as we had continued to pray over the years for God to remake him into our vision of a well-formed and healthy child. We had somewhat selfishly asked God to redo His handiwork when we should have been accepting of God's plan for his life and trusting that the Father who loves us wants only what is best for him.

If you follow the will of God, you know that in spite of all the terrible things that happen to you, you will never lose a final refuge. You know that the foundation of the world is love, so that even when no human being can or will help you, you may go on, trusting in the One that loves you.
Pope Benedict XVI, *Jesus of Nazareth*

Over the years, acknowledging this has been both humbling and illuminating as I have thought about how to apply the virtue of acceptance into other areas of my life. These years of reflection have made me realize how often without thinking I ask God for His help in improving situations and solving problems. Instead of praying for acceptance and discernment about what lessons God wants to teach me or the blessings hidden in these challenges, I seek to reshape the issues into something more pleasing to me instead of pleasing to Him.

Do you ever fall into the "acceptance trap" as well? Perhaps these questions can help you reframe your thinking:

- Are you open to seeing career setbacks as learning opportunities to help you grow and learn?
- Do you see opportunities for growth in the adversity and struggle of everyday life?
- Does illness (yours or others) offer opportunities to transform suffering into a blessing?
- Do you see financial challenges as an opportunity to be more grateful for your faith, family, friendships and a deeper appreciation for a simpler life that allows you to live within your means?

As St. Paul says, "I consider that the sufferings of this present time are as nothing compared with the glory to be revealed for us" (Romans 8:18). It is often difficult to see the blessings and good in any kind of suffering, yet we know from the earliest Church teaching there is redemptive power in suffering if we learn to give it up to God. Practicing the virtue of acceptance may require a radical recalibration of our mindsets as well as complete trust and faith in God's plan for our lives. We must be faithful, humble, patient, obedient and prayerful if we are to learn the lessons and blessings God has in store for us in our daily trials. We must also seek to glorify Him and not ourselves through the way we deal with challenges and always express our gratitude for the good and the bad that comes our way.

> *We always find that those who walked closest to Christ were those who had to bear the greatest trials.*
> St. Teresa of Avila

I can look back now and see the tremendous positive influence our oldest son has had on our family. His diagnosis with autism more than twenty-five years ago and the challenges this presented began the long and often difficult process of lowering the wall around my closed-off heart. In the summer of 2005, we moved into the area where we now live to be closer to his school and therapists. This move began a chain of life-changing events that eventually led to our family joining the Catholic Church later that year. The opening of my heart which began at his diagnosis allowed me to experience a profound conversion experience in September 2005 when I finally surrendered to Christ and put aside the pride and stubbornness that had dominated my life for so long. Without a doubt, our gifted child and his presence in our lives was a significant catalyst behind our joining the Church and the strong faith our family has today.

Maybe this was God's plan all along for our son, and I know my wife and I were specifically chosen out of all the parents in the world to be his parents. I am just grateful that I can see it now and accept him, not only as one of my wonderful children whom I love, but also as a child of God given to us for His divine purpose.

ACCEPTANCE

Perhaps in this crazy world in which we live, we can all more thoughtfully practice acceptance of God's will and see the challenges in our lives as blessings, not burdens.

Heavenly Father, I humbly ask that you grant me the gift of acceptance today. Please help me to understand the lessons and blessings hidden within the challenges my family and I will face and know that I am grateful to you for our lives and the incredible gift and sacrifice of your Son, Jesus Christ. Amen.

How does this idea of acceptance speak to you? In your own life, do you possibly have an opportunity to accept and appreciate your own difficult circumstances and challenges as blessings and learning experiences instead of burdens?

CHAPTER 2

Accountability

Taking Ownership and Accelerating Your Career

Responsibility is a grace you give yourself, not an obligation.
Dan Millman, author

I will be forever grateful that my parents taught me to work hard and be responsible, and these and other priceless gifts they shared when I lived under their roof have largely shaped who I am today. In the early stages of my career, I was also fortunate to have wise mentors who guided me, challenged me, and shared invaluable advice that helped me get off to a strong start in the first several years after I graduated from college. If there was one key lesson from that formative period that stands out for me and served as a catalyst for accelerating my career, it was embracing the virtue of *accountability*.

The virtue of accountability means taking ownership of your actions, decisions, and mistakes, and demonstrating that you are reliable by following through on commitments. It is about actively contributing to achieving team and company goals, which builds trust and credibility within your professional network and fosters the growth of your career. In the early years out of college, it is easy to feel overwhelmed by all you must learn as you adapt to a new business culture and navigate relationships, but the one thing completely in your control is the degree of ownership you show in your daily work—your willingness to be held accountable for your actions and results.

What are best practices to help early career professionals embrace accountability? I offer these ten actionable ideas from my experience and observation over the years that are proven approaches to make you more accountable.

1. **Become more self-aware.** Look in the mirror and reflect on your strengths and weaknesses to determine where you can improve your accountability.
2. **Take responsibility.** Own up to errors, admit when you don't know something, and actively seek solutions to correct mistakes.
3. **Clarify expectations.** Make sure you fully understand what is being asked of you and when it is due. The worst thing you can do is work on a project without a full understanding of what your boss really wants and deliver a work product that is not aligned with those expectations. Being curious and asking probing questions is key.
4. **Always meet deadlines.** Consistently deliver work on time and according to expectations of your

supervisor. Missed deadlines will damage your credibility as we discuss in Chapter 8.

5. **Communicate frequently.** Keep your work colleagues informed about progress, challenges, and potential roadblocks—no surprises.
6. **Be transparent.** Be open and honest about your work, including areas where you might need support. The worst thing you can do is struggle in silence.
7. **Be proactive.** Identify issues early on and take initiative to find solutions. Experience and increasing self-confidence will be your allies here.
8. **Actively seek out mentors.** Growing in the virtue of accountability is almost impossible without mentors who are willing to candidly advise and guide you. Seek out people who know more than you, have credibility and respect, and are likely more senior and have a proven track record. Humbly ask for their time and seek their help. Helpful tip: Show great respect for these relationships, make the most of them, and honor their investment in you. Be committed and show gratitude.
9. **Consistently seek candid feedback.** Actively seek specific and unbiased feedback from mentors, supervisors, and peers to improve your performance. Don't always seek affirmation and validation, but instead develop a real appreciation for hearing the difficult comments about how

you are doing to dramatically improve your performance. Embrace critical feedback as an opportunity for growth and do not view it as a personal attack.
10. **Be a great team player.** Actively support your teammates in attaining their personal goals and the team's goals. Be a great collaborator. Selflessly do what you can to help them and hold them accountable—and seek the same from them.

What is the payoff? What will you gain from this investment in being more accountable? I would suggest these are the four key benefits you can expect from embracing this virtue:

1. **You will accelerate your career.** Demonstrating accountability can lead to increased responsibilities and career progression. This will set you apart from many of your peers and give you an edge.
2. **You will foster trusting relationships.** Being accountable builds greater trust with colleagues, clients, and supervisors, leading to stronger working relationships.
3. **You will enhance your reputation.** Building a reputation for accountability can elevate an early career professional's personal brand within the team, company, and industry.
4. **You will experience significant personal growth.** Cultivating the virtue of accountability and being

responsible through reflecting on your actions encourages continuous learning and development. This mindset will serve you well throughout your career.

I am also reminded of the advice I received early in my career from a wise mentor: "If you touch it, you own it. Even if you only have 1 percent of the actual problem/issue, act as if you have 100 percent. If we all act this way, our work gets done faster and our problems are quickly solved." When used with discernment, a collaborative mindset, and good judgment, this is invaluable advice.

I hope these actionable best practices foster within you a much greater appreciation for accountability and the positive effect it will have on your life and career. Growing in the virtue of accountability not only profoundly impacts your career but also positively impacts your personal life as well. Your family, friends, and community will also benefit from your commitment to being more accountable.

How would rate your embrace of the virtue of accountability right now on a scale of one to ten? Based on the best practices offered here, where do you need to improve? Do you have mentors and other colleagues who can help you? If not, where will you find them? Over the next thirty days, develop a personal plan to fully activate these best practices in your daily life and add other ideas that may be working for you.

CHAPTER 3

Authenticity

Let's Be Real

֎

To be yourself in a world that is constantly trying to make you something else is the greatest accomplishment.
Ralph Waldo Emerson

I have discussed the virtue of authenticity with other business professionals for decades. Over the last few years, these conversations have migrated from the importance of allowing others to see the "real" us to guarded discussions about the increasing anxiety people have in today's world regarding being open about and advocating for their beliefs and convictions. In a few very recent discussions with other business leaders, I received blank stares and obvious discomfort when I advocated for being the same person no matter where we were and transparent about our lives with others. *Why is authenticity so uncomfortable?*

I suspect the root cause of this occurred for many of us at a young age. The first time we felt pressure to "fit in" with a particular group in school, we began down the path of conformity that only accelerated as we grew older. In college, we may have heard from professors (or parents) that we need to keep our work, faith, beliefs, and personal lives separate. We may have feared being judged or criticized in those early jobs for sharing anything personal, which only hardens into a compartmentalized mindset as we grow in our careers.

Logic should tell us it is inevitably harmful to suppress our true selves for a sustained period of time, yet people may sometimes feel there is no other option. Do you love being a parent but feel awkward about discussing your kids and home life at work? Do you care passionately about a particular cause but refrain from mentioning it for fear of condemnation? Have you struggled with a personal challenge and felt the need to hide it from colleagues lest they judge you? Have you been faced with a difficult situation that conflicts with your principles and values, but remained silent rather than risking criticism? I suspect most of us, me included, have faced these kinds of situations. I choose to believe that deep down most of us desire to be more consistently authentic, but we may not know how to get there.

Obstacles to Authenticity

Let's address some of the obstacles that may prevent you from being authentic. I am making a basic assumption that you agree on some level that authenticity is important and have a desire to be more open, transparent, and genuine. In my experience, here are some of the obstacles that can inhibit authenticity:

AUTHENTICITY

- **Lack of self-awareness**—Do you even know there's a problem?
- **Fear** of people not liking who you truly are. Fear of not fitting in. Fear of being judged. Fear of persecution for your principles and beliefs. Fear of being passed over for a promotion because you don't fit the corporate mold. Fear of being "canceled" in today's culture.
- **Lack of courage** in defending your opinions and convictions.
- **Attachment** to an income level and lifestyle that requires unhealthy compromise.
- **Conforming** to society's march toward political correctness, restrictions on free speech, and acceptance of things that are in direct conflict with your values and principles.
- **Relaxing your moral standards** because it easier to go along with the crowd than take a stand.
- **Incorrectly believing** that presenting your generic or "fake" self in the workplace is the only path to success.
- **Lack of role models, mentors, and candid friends** who can show you the right approach and help you improve in this area.

This list may be as painful for you to acknowledge as it was for me to write—or you may have a different list. The points raised may be unsettling, but confronting them is necessary if you are to pursue and embrace a more authentic life.

How Do We Overcome These Obstacles?

One way forward is to open the aperture about *how* we view the practice of authenticity. It is not enough to simply be authentic; we also have a responsibility to help authenticity thrive in others. Here are **nine positive ways** we can *demonstrate* and *promote* authenticity in daily life:

1. **Treat others with kindness, gratitude, mercy, compassion, fairness, and love.** These can all be powerful manifestations of authenticity if they emanate from our core beliefs and reflect how we truly feel about others.
2. **Be respectful and civil.** I interact with professionals every day who may fundamentally disagree with me on a number of topics, but I always try to respect their points of view, and I ask for that same respect in return. We share our perspectives, experiences, and beliefs in a civil discussion rooted in mutual respect.
3. **Replace angry political arguments with civil discussions about *ideas*.** Let's promote the lost concept of healthy debates. We need more calm dialogue and less screaming in today's polarized world.
4. **Practice active listening.** Good listening skills are essential for promoting authenticity. This is especially true if we make the choice to listen to conflicting opinions with calmness. We should consider responding with thoughtful questions before offering our own opinions in return. If we are truly listening

AUTHENTICITY

with a desire to learn, we must keep an open mind and even be willing to change our opinion if warranted.

5. **Diversity of opinion is a good thing.** Conflicting views, beliefs, and opinions contribute to diversity of thought. Without it we risk a frightening monolithic worldview where everyone thinks the same way.
6. **Transparency invites transparency.** Be transparent first. Get personal. If we desire someone to open up to us, we should be open about our lives first. In effect, by sharing first we give the other person "permission" to be open about nonwork-related topics.
7. **Be curious.** Be insatiably curious about others. Learn and remember personal things about them, such as their spouse and kid's names, hobbies, interests, and birthdays. Open-ended questions like "Where did you grow up?", "What did you do this weekend?", or "What are you doing for vacation this summer?" can be a great way to begin. Authenticity is greatly enhanced by mutual sharing and sharing thrives in an atmosphere of curiosity.
8. **Build a foundation of trust.** Business relationships will become stronger and more meaningful when you allow others to know, like, and trust you.
9. **Read the room.** Being consistently authentic does not mean always sharing our sad stories or deeply emotional experiences. It does not mean we should share every aspect of our personal lives or topics inappropriate for a particular audience or situation. Use good judgment. Read the room. Be smart.

We must challenge the fear that somehow being real is a bad thing. It may be uncomfortable and create some opposition in the short term from individuals not used to it. However, practicing transparency, engaging in honest and open dialogue, and always placing our principles and ethics before advancing our careers will bring us greater success in every aspect of our lives. I have seen the positive fruits of this in my own life and the lives of countless other business leaders. *I would also argue that the most authentic business leaders I know are also the most inspiring and by far the most successful.*

I am sharing this from my perspective as a father, husband, person of faith, and business owner who is very involved in the community. You may have different perspectives and views on this topic, but I believe anyone can find relevant value in what I am sharing. Maybe we should stop thinking that being ourselves, holding differing views on important subjects, or resisting the expectations of the surrounding culture are somehow bad things. In the business world, we should all seek the freedom to no longer sacrifice our uniqueness and who we truly are on the altar of political expediency.

After you read this chapter, take some time to consider if you are being authentic to those around you. Commit to setting a good example for others, especially the generations coming after you, by being unafraid to be your true self. Remember that a lifetime of little compromises at work (and elsewhere) eventually adds up to an overwhelming denial of who we really are. Authenticity is not easy, but it's necessary if we want to change the growing challenges around the simple practice of being our real selves. Our virtuous acts of authenticity in the workplace, exercised with *prudence* and good judgment, can dramatically improve the quality of business conversations, foster trusting relationships, unleash hidden potential, and potentially improve business results.

With confidence and a sense of purpose, let's all try to be a little more authentic to the people around us.

How will you show up as more authentic to the people in your life, beginning tomorrow?

CHAPTER 4

Candor

A Road Map to Candid Work Conversations

દે

Great teams do not hold back with one another. They are unafraid to air their dirty laundry. They admit their mistakes, their weaknesses, and their concerns without fear of reprisal.
PATRICK LENCIONI, *The Five Dysfunctions of a Team*

You're in a staff meeting listening to a work colleague drone on about his success on a recent project, but you know he is actually behind and over budget. What do you do?

You are a first-time manager, and one of your direct reports has a few self-limiting behaviors that are impeding her career growth and negatively affecting the team, but you don't want to hurt her feelings. Performance reviews are coming up, and you need to rate her work. *How will you handle the situation?*

A colleague lacks self-awareness about the negative reputation he has earned in the company. You have no obligation to do so, but you want to help him get back on track. *How will you approach him?*

One of your company's senior executives consistently asks for feedback, but you doubt his sincerity. A business problem arises that you know will reflect poorly on decisions made by this leader. *Will you have the courage to speak up?*

I observe and hear about scenarios like these playing out in companies nearly every day. Direct, honest feedback about performance and other important topics has become a lost art in many corporate environments, and this has given way to coddling, surface conversations, and conflict workarounds. A pervasive lack of candid conversations in business has a significant negative psychological, cultural, and financial impact on leaders, teams, and entire organizations when left unaddressed. Lack of candor causes distrust, stifles innovation, slows decision-making, and hampers productivity. The desire to avoid conflict is understandable, but it's one of the most debilitating factors in business today, and this behavior exacts a steep price. If the problem is as widespread as I believe it to be, what do we do about it?

Why Is the Virtue of Candor Difficult?

Let's make an effort to understand why we have a candor problem in the workplace today. I have identified **five key causes**:

1. **Lack of self-awareness:** Are you and I aware that we might have a problem in this area? Has anyone told us? Are we sincerely seeking critical and honest feedback about how we come across to others?
2. **PC work environments:** A too-polite veneer often signals an overly politicized workplace. Colleagues who are afraid to speak honestly to people's faces often

do it behind their backs. A fear of saying the wrong thing or being misunderstood by those around us has placed a significant restriction on meaningful dialogue in today's workplace and instead often encourages surface conversations at the expense of candid ones.
3. **Fear of hurting the feelings of others:** Candor is typically and incorrectly assumed to be negative or hurtful instead of the helpful gift it truly is when delivered well. We may struggle to navigate the tension between delivering an honest and helpful message versus hurting the feelings of our colleagues.
4. **Fear of repercussions:** If I am candid and say the wrong thing to the wrong person, what will happen to me? Will my career growth or even my job be at risk if I speak up?
5. **Not sure what to say:** Surprisingly, this is one of the most common obstacles to speaking with more candor at work. I find that many well-intentioned professionals desire to speak more candidly with their colleagues, but they wish to do it in a way that will be accepted with minimal frustration and pain. They simply lack the words and overthink what should necessarily be a respectful, clear, and helpful conversation.

Embrace New Concepts and Approaches

When I shared with a friend my intention to write on this topic, he assumed it would be some sort of "Candor Manifesto" meant to move every company's culture in the direction of increased candor. I am skeptical of company-wide initiatives of this magnitude and instead place my faith in the sincere efforts of individuals who are willing to embrace healthy and meaningful change. You see, I believe the best way to positively impact our work cultures and make candor more attractive is through the intentional actions of each reader of this book. If each of us will subscribe to the "pebble in a pond" concept, our individual embrace and application of candor will ripple throughout our organizations. We must model the behavior we wish to see in everybody else. How do we do this? First, I would encourage each of us to consider these basic concepts:

- Candid conversations do *not* have to be ugly or painful.
- All candid feedback, if given respectfully, is a gift. "Candor is a compliment; it implies equality. It's how true friends talk," says Peggy Noonan, author and Wall Street Journal columnist.
- If we assume good intent and think of the person giving us honest feedback as helpful and generous rather than critical, we become less defensive and more open to changing our behavior.
- In order to initiate effective candid conversations, let's try to orient our thinking this way: "I desire to be helpful, and I care enough about you to tell you the truth."
- Candid conversations are best served with clear, simple, direct language that includes relevant examples. The calling card of dishonest talk is flowery or ambiguous language.

CANDOR

There are numerous misperceptions about candor, and we often have an unhealthy fear of what it is and is not. In fact, I would argue that candor is a helpful weapon against fear and not something in itself to be feared. *Candor* comes from the Latin word *candere*, which means "to shine or illuminate." Perhaps to practice the virtue of candor means we must be courageous enough to shine a light into dark places. Embracing the concepts above is part of the solution, but we need to also be intentional about changing our behaviors.

Twelve Best Practices for Facilitating Candid Work Conversations

1. **Model it.** Be willing to model the behavior you wish to see in others. Are you setting a good and consistent example for those around you? Do you both speak with candor and receive it well from others?
2. **Admit mistakes.** One of the best ways to begin a candid conversation is to be humble enough to admit you've made a mistake and own the consequences. How often do we see leaders do this today?
3. **Never punish; always reward.** Don't shoot the messenger! If someone has the courage to speak up about uncomfortable topics, publicly acknowledge and thank them for their honesty. Encourage others to follow their example.
4. **Be courteous and ask permission.** Whenever I need to deliver what may be taken as difficult feedback, I ask permission first. I simply say, "May I have permission to be candid?" In all the years I have asked

this question, nobody has ever said no. The other person enters into a psychological "contract" with me, knowing I am going to share something they may not like, but they appreciate my courtesy and are prepared to receive what I wish to share.

5. **Give permission.** Let everyone around you know you are sincerely open to hearing their candid thoughts. Rather than putting someone on the spot and asking for feedback (which often inspires anxiety), try giving those around you blanket permission to come to you in private when they have something to share. When receiving candid feedback, always thank the person who offered it and avoid being defensive.

6. **Be respectful.** An offshoot of my fourth point about asking for permission is to always be respectful of your audience if you wish your message to be more readily accepted. Egos can be easily bruised in these exchanges and being respectful is a great best practice you can utilize to defuse the tension your directness may cause. You should both deliver and receive messages this way. Use phrases like "Are you open to a different perspective?", "I might suggest . . . ," or "Please consider this . . ." when offering feedback. Where applicable, express sincere praise for things done well in addition to giving feedback on challenges or ways to improve.

7. **Be constructive and helpful.** Negative feedback can sometimes hurt, but learn to view it is a gift aimed at helping the recipient improve performance and

avoid future mistakes. One way to be more helpful is to be clear about the challenging behaviors you have observed and the suggestions you offer for improvement. Stay away from ambiguous language and use concrete examples whenever possible.

8. **Avoid embarrassment.** It will sometimes be necessary in meetings to have difficult conversations with your colleagues, so be mindful that you do not want to embarrass them while still delivering an honest and helpful message. There is a huge difference between picking projects apart and picking people apart.

9. **Be more curious.** We often miss opportunities for candid and substantive conversations because we fail to ask questions and show genuine curiosity. Asking probing questions of others rather than merely stating our opinions can often provide an opportunity to bring difficult topics to light. Examples can look like this: "Mike, do you feel like you are having the kind of success you hoped for in your new role?" or "Sarah, I am concerned that you might miss your goals this quarter. What do you see as the obstacles in your way and how can I help you overcome them?"

10. **Candor is best when delivered in person.** As a rule, nothing that is emotional, awkward, or subject to misinterpretation should ever be conveyed via email or text. Candor is best suited to in-person conversations, video calls, or by phone if necessary. If it all possible, I would encourage delivering candid feedback in private to ensure maximum receptivity.

11. **Promote candor through team accountability.** Real collaboration is unlikely to occur when people don't trust one another to speak with candor. Suggest to your teammates that candor be strongly encouraged in every team or staff meeting and be sure to model it for others. Recommend taking turns holding one another accountable for this behavior and do not be afraid to respectfully call out your colleagues when someone avoids addressing difficult issues.
12. **No jerks allowed.** There is no place for bullying or boorish behavior in this vision of a candid workplace. Demeaning our colleagues in any way should not be tolerated in cultures that claim to value their employees.

In my own experience, I have found that my effectiveness in having candid conversations with anyone is predicated on the other person trusting that I am sincerely trying to be helpful. I own the responsibility to earn that trust, and I do so through investing heavily in building authentic relationships with my business network. There are no tricks, gimmicks, or hidden agendas, but there is a lot of hard work (as illustrated by the twelve best practices above) to ensure that I am doing my part in encouraging mutually respectful candid conversations. These conversations provide a great opportunity to apply the Golden Rule and treat others as I wish to be treated.

The Fruits of Candor and a Call to Action

If you sincerely implement these best practices with consistency, people in all areas of your life will begin to seek you out for insights and advice because they can count on you to deliver what so few people in their circles are willing to provide. Whether you are a subordinate or a manager, the key is to take some sort of action to increase the candor and flow of honest dialogue in your organization. If you do nothing, you are just reinforcing unproductive patterns. But if you are willing to do *something*, you can help trigger a cycle of increasing self-awareness, personal growth, and elevated performance for yourself and others—and create a much more enjoyable and trusting work environment for everyone.

Professionals at any stage in their career who intentionally embrace the virtue of candor will encourage, and even reward, straight talk from their colleagues and teams. They understand that whatever momentary discomfort they may experience is more than offset by the fact that better information and honest conversations help them operate more effectively and make better decisions. *Unfortunately, there is no easy way to institutionalize candor on a large scale.* Candid behavior at the top of the leadership chain is critical, but lasting change in this area requires sustained effort, focus, and constant vigilance from each of us, regardless of our title. It also requires a sincere willingness to own our behavior and make the necessary changes. This is the clear challenge I am asking each of us to accept as a positive step toward making an impactful difference in our workplaces today.

Will you take on the "candor challenge"?
Commit to these three helpful steps:

PRACTICAL VIRTUE

- *Identify and reflect on why candor may be difficult for you.*
- *Practice at least three of these candor best practices each week.*
- *Continue practicing them until you have mastered them all.*

CHAPTER 5

Civility

Fostering Greater Civility

∽

*Let me never fall into the vulgar mistake of dreaming that
I am persecuted whenever I am contradicted.*
RALPH WALDO EMERSON

I was surprised by a call I received a few weeks before I finished the manuscript for my 2022 book, *Upon Reflection*, from someone I have known for a few years. We have a few friends in common, do similar work, and bump into each other on occasion, but we would consider each other professional acquaintances and not friends. When we finished pleasantries, I asked him what I could do for him, and he responded, "You are one of the few people I think I can trust to give me an honest opinion on a controversial topic, and I would like to ask you a few questions if you are open to it." Intrigued, I told him I would be glad to help and listened intently to what he had to say.

He shared that based on what he knew about me from my

writings and our mutual friends, he assumed I would have firm opinions about a very contentious topic that has caused anger and division in our country for many years. He said he respected me and was very eager to hear my perspective. He admitted that he probably had the opposite view on the topic, but he wanted to understand where I was coming from and increase his level of understanding. I confirmed his assumption about my opinion and calmly shared my perspective. I carefully walked through my reasoning with him, gave him context, and shared a few clear examples to emphasize my point. He asked a few questions along the way and seemed to be cautiously avoiding sounding defensive or frustrated. When I was finished, I asked him to explain his reasoning to help me understand his point of view as well.

The same conversation played out in reverse as he calmly walked me through his perspective, giving examples and sharing context. He genuinely seemed to appreciate my questions and before we knew it, our conversation had gone on for nearly an hour. I was admittedly surprised that we calmly listened to each other and exhibited mutual respect. Although there was probably some tension below the surface because of the nature of the topic, we were careful to keep our emotions in check and restrained any animosity we both may have felt.

There was an awkward silence when he finished until I said aloud what we were both likely thinking: "What just happened?"

He shared that he was sick of the anger and divisiveness that has caused so much polarization in our country and decided to do something that was decidedly countercultural—hence his call to me. I agreed wholeheartedly and thanked him for the courage, calmness, and civility he showed in reaching out. I know I will not change my opinion on this particular topic, and I suspect he won't change his either, but we will agree to disagree, knowing we both heard each other out and improved our mutual understanding. We kept on chatting for another thirty minutes and were surprised to learn that we also had much in common. We agreed to continue the conversation over coffee in the coming weeks, and I sincerely look forward to the discussion with someone who may become a new friend.

Why Does This Matter?

I think we have all observed, hopefully with great concern, that difficult conversations like the one I just described rarely occur anymore. You see people's opinions dismissed or belittled because of their political or religious affiliation, the color of their skin, their gender, and other various reasons. There is a tendency to go from zero to angry when difficult and contentious topics are raised, with both sides pointing fingers and voices being raised . . . or senseless violence being the unfortunate result. There was a time when we debated ideas, shared different opinions, and found ways to compromise and collaborate for the greater good in our country. Are those days long gone? Will they ever return?

We may disagree with one another on a number of things, but we must respect one another's perspective and one another's right to share that perspective in a calm and reasonable way. Any person or group who tries to shut down discussion and the debate of ideas and thoughts makes themselves resemble tyrants and dictators who can't defend the hollowness and errors of their thinking. I think reasonable people have had enough.

A Road Map to Live the Virtue of Civility

The call I referred to at the beginning of the chapter holds many keys to improving how we approach the virtue of civility. Here are seven additional ideas to consider as you engage in future potentially difficult conversations:

1. **Start with mutual respect and courtesy.** The gentleman who reached out to me set the tone with respect and courtesy at the very beginning of our conversation, and it made a huge difference in our ability to have a calm and reasonable discussion. We also both chose to be personable and friendly, not disagreeable.
2. **Actively listen.** One of the greatest catalysts for productive conversations is to actively listen and show understanding. Don't impatiently listen until it is your turn to speak. Listen to understand the other person's point of view. "The greatest compliment that was ever paid me was when someone asked me what I thought and attended to my answer" (Henry David Thoreau).
3. **Free speech is a fundamental right for all, even if you don't like what someone says.** In a quote often erroneously attributed to Voltaire, Evelyn Beatrice Hall

wrote: "I disapprove of what you say, but I will defend to the death your right to say it." You may not like what the other person is saying, but they absolutely have a right to say it, as do we all.

4. **You might learn something new.** Try being more curious and ask thoughtful questions. If you approach conversations with a desire to learn, you might gain new perspectives and deeper understanding. You might even change your mind.

5. **Keep emotions in check.** This one can feel very challenging, especially during a contentious discussion on a difficult topic. Being animated and fully engaged is just fine, but be mindful when anger and frustration bubble to the surface and work hard to keep these emotions in check.

6. **Social media is not conducive to civil discussions.** I received a phone call that resulted in a ninety-minute discussion on a tough topic. We vetted the contentious topic thoroughly from all angles in a calm and respectful manner. A frustrated tweet or angry Facebook post will only invite vitriol and a series of "gotcha" comments. Get on the phone or meet in person if at all possible!

7. **Sometimes you have to be courageous.** The call I received was an act of courage. This man had no idea how I would react or the outcome of our conversation. It will take increased acts of courage like this and more of us bravely stepping up if we are going to tilt the scales back toward civility.

I am not the expert on the virtue of civility, and I need to work on this like many of us. I believe, as I hope you will agree, that we have more in common with one another than we are often willing to admit. Let's sit down and calmly reason together rather than assume the worst of one another. If someone disagrees with us, we have an opportunity to listen, share, thoughtfully persuade them, or maybe just agree to disagree—and hopefully not get frustrated, become angry, and walk away. Our anger and frustration should *never* lead to breaking the law or violence of any kind. As I've shared before in other writings, G. K. Chesterton said it best: "We men and women are all in the same boat upon a stormy sea. We owe to each other a terrible and tragic loyalty."

Promoting and modeling the virtue of civility at work, home, and the community starts with you and me. Let's embrace the challenge.

Consider how you view the level of civility around you. How can you make a difference in promoting and living the virtue of civility over the next few weeks? What will you do differently based on the seven ideas you just read?

CHAPTER 6

Clarity

Getting Clarity Right

☙

*Clarity is the preoccupation of the effective leader.
If you do nothing else as a leader, be clear.*
MARCUS BUCKINGHAM

As I began writing this chapter, I reflected on the conversations I have been having with clients and other business leaders over the past few years. I was struck by a central theme that seems to be popping up in most of them: the importance of *clarity* and the negative impact the lack of clarity has on teams and organizations. A simple way to define the virtue of clarity is the ability to make sense of things and help others do the same. The primary reason this issue is hitting my radar is a key question I ask my clients every January: "What are the biggest challenges for you and your team that you wish to address more effectively this year?" Consistently, I hear a desire to improve accountability, increase efficiency, foster greater ownership, improve communication, and achieve better overall results. I would suggest the answer to all of these challenges—or at least the beginning of the answer—can be found by dramatically improving and consistently practicing the virtue of clarity.

Why is clarity so difficult to consistently achieve? One big reason is that we may be too busy racing from task to task rather than thoughtfully creating clarity in our spheres of influence at work and requiring clarity from others. *Why are we so busy?* Perhaps it is because we are negatively affected by the inefficiency created by the lack of clarity and the dysfunctional way it takes over our calendars with repetitive meetings and calls to rehash the same conversations over and over (visualize a hamster on a flywheel). Perhaps we have accepted the lack of clarity as "the way we do things around here." Maybe, just maybe, the challenge with clarity is connected to a lack of *candor*. Are we willing to clearly and publicly identify issues in front of our colleagues and commit to greater accountability with deadlines? Are we willing to respectfully but candidly question how we do things within our teams and organizations in an effort to make them better?

If clarity is an issue for us, our teams, and our companies, how do we address it? Let's begin by focusing on **five types of clarity** that can positively impact decision-making, the way business meetings are conducted, overall efficiency, and execution:

1. **Do we have clarity around the "why"?** Why is this project necessary and what will it solve? Why are we having this meeting? Is there an agenda and do we know why we are here and what we need to get done?

The "why" question is the most important and can be applied to almost every action and decision. If we can clearly answer the "why," can we connect it back to our overall strategy? Consider how you can better incorporate the "why" question into your daily routine and connect it to better outcomes with the people you encounter each day.

2. **Do we have clarity on tasks and deadlines?** What specifically are we asking others to do? What are the details? When exactly is the assignment/task due? For example, sending someone into battle to "hurry up and fix the company sales problem" is setting them up for failure. We need to marry specificity to actions and tasks, including clear deadlines. Consider this example: "Mike will be creating a process to increase revenue by 5 percent in professional services before the end of Q2 and will have his action plan on how to do this ready to present in our next staff meeting." Doing this aspect of clarity well is directly connected to dramatically improving accountability.

3. **Do we have clarity on expectations?** I love this leadership communication principle often taught by my business partner Brandon Smith: "Dysfunction is like a fungus . . . it lives in dark places. Clarify your expectations to eliminate it."

    Common Examples
    - "I need more collaboration from your team." (Unclear)
    - "I got part of what I needed from you, but I

assumed you would have handled part three as well." (Assumption)
- "Your team just needs to move faster." (Unclear)
- "This is OK, but I would have done it differently." (Assumption)
- "We will miss our goal if your team doesn't kick it into a higher gear." (Unclear)

Poorly defined expectations, assumptions, and lack of candor can cause havoc on any team. Be clear, be candid, stop assuming people can read your mind, and recap your expectations of others in writing.

4. **Do we have role clarity?** This aspect of clarity goes beyond task ownership and is more about defining the sandbox we will play in, what we are accountable for, and how we will specifically do our job, contribute to a project, or help in solving a problem faced by the team. Role clarity also defines the overall scope and responsibilities of our job. There will always be some unavoidable degree of overlap in certain roles, but an emphasis on clarifying roles, duties, and decision-making rights (in writing) can make this problem more palatable and reduce unnecessary friction. As you ponder this point, do you have role clarity in your current position?

5. **Do we have clarity of communication?** Ambiguity and overall lack of clarity in leadership communication often contributes to misunderstandings, inefficiency, and poor execution. *Every email or text from a leader needs to create clarity, not confusion or chaos.* Who is my audience? What am I trying to convey? Have I given them clear action

steps? Did I explain the "why"? The thoughts below are primarily associated with improving business meetings, but I am focusing on this because most of the communication dysfunction I observe takes place in poorly run meetings and the resulting follow-up. Consider this short list of action steps for every business meeting:

- Never have a meeting without a clear agenda, ideally shared forty-eight hours in advance.
- Always assign a scribe to take notes (rotate this assignment within the team), specifically listing a summary of key points from the meeting, task ownership, the specific tasks in detail, and due dates.
- Disseminate meeting notes to all participants within twenty-four hours of meeting.

I recognize this may seem like a lot of hard work when you are likely very busy. But I encourage you to consider that embracing the virtue of clarity will actually reduce your workload, make you more efficient, and enhance your ability to execute. If you have become the proverbial hamster on the flywheel, it is time to get off.

Keep at it, and the clarity you can offer those within your sphere of influence *will* improve.

How can you quickly make progress on how you practice the virtue of clarity? Here are practical approaches to try, beginning this week:

PRACTICAL VIRTUE

- *Are you good at clarity? Ask for candid feedback from colleagues.*
- *Ask yourself each of the five clarity questions posed in this chapter before big decisions, certainly before and during every meeting, and before communicating with your colleagues.*
- *Create space on your calendar to be more thoughtful about clarity.*
- *Don't worry if your attempts at clarity are not perfect. Focus on simply making the effort and go for small wins.*
- *Frequently discuss the topic with your colleagues in meetings and promote greater accountability to get it right.*
- *Try to be the role model for everyone else.*
- *Always remember that every email, call, meeting, and decision has a ripple effect and real consequences. Please reflect on this and act accordingly . . . with a commitment to practice the virtue of clarity top of mind.*

CHAPTER 7

Commitment

Facing Veracruz Moments

Most people fail not because of a lack of desire but because of a lack of commitment.
VINCE LOMBARDI

As you may recall from history, the Spanish conquistador Hernan Cortes and his small army of six hundred men landed in Veracruz, Mexico, in 1519 with dreams of conquering the mighty Aztec empire. Many of his men were afraid and filled with doubts in the face of such a daunting mission, so Cortes made the decision to *burn their ships*. With retreat now impossible and no place to go except forward to face their enemy, his men were properly motivated and fully committed to fulfill their mission.

Many of my clients deal with the challenge of embracing the virtue of commitment, and I have certainly had my own numerous encounters with it over my career. Being fully committed means being "all in" and can include the way we approach big strategic decisions, how much effort we are willing to contribute to a project, leaving our job for a new one, or even starting a new business. Commitment can also pertain to more personal aspects of life, such as getting married, buying a home, exercise, our prayer lives, eating better, or dropping bad habits.

When I launched my company Serviam Partners in 2012, I had to overcome my own risk aversion to be fully committed and "burn my ships." I could not fail as my family was depending on me, so I put everything I had into ensuring my business would be successful. *There was no going back.* The same is true of the Leadership Foundry, which I co-founded with Brandon Smith in 2018. We started small and carefully refined our model, feeling confident it would be successful. After lots of committed effort, we are thrilled that this fast-growing business we love continues to thrive.

As much as I believe in the power of full commitment and being decisive, I also recognize that good contingency planning and cultivating multiple options is also prudent in business and life. This might apply to most of the decisions we make on any given day. But, as I hope you will agree, there are going to be critical moments in our lives where we need to be 100 percent committed and hold nothing back. The ships may have to be burned in these critical moments, and we can't hedge our bets.

What Gets in the Way?

I believe there is one primary obstacle (that surpasses all other obstacles). That obstacle is a thought—the thought that if things don't work out, we will always have an escape plan to fall back on. Knowing we have an escape plan prevents us from giving every ounce of effort needed for true success, achieving difficult goals, or making meaningful changes in our lives.

What can we do to grow our practice of the virtue of commitment and more readily embrace our "Veracruz moments"? Here are **four ideas**:

1. **Get accountability partners.** They can help keep you on track, challenge you, and encourage you. Find someone who will not let you off the hook for giving less than a total effort and full commitment to whatever you are trying to do.
2. **Don't struggle in silence.** If faced with "Veracruz moments," ask for help. Get advice from trusted friends and mentors. Do your homework. Don't face these big decisions alone. Chances are, someone you know has been through something similar in their own life and can offer invaluable insights and perspectives.
3. **Make bold public goals.** I have often found this to be a useful mind trick to help me accomplish big goals or projects. Here is an example: When I am writing a series of blog posts, I share the title of the next post that will come out the following week. Most of the time, this new post is not yet written, and I am highly motivated to write it to honor my weekly public announcement (commitment). It's a simple trick, but it works for me.
4. **Be clear about the worthiness of the outcome you**

seek. Having a clear understanding of the worthiness of the outcomes you desire in any area of your life can often properly motivate you to be all in. For example, you may be nervous about taking ownership of a new project at work, but you know the project will fail unless you lead it.

If you agree that being all in at the appropriate times is important, what are the fruits of this total commitment? Here are **three positive outcomes** I have observed in the lives of others and in my own experience:

1. **Clarity of purpose:** You are single-minded about your goal(s) and fully aware of *why* you are making the effort. Also, the hoped-for outcome and the hard work connected to your commitment level exist in relative harmony.
2. **Focused, efficient, and effective:** When you are all in, you are able to more efficiently apply your energy and resources toward a single effort versus hedging your bets on multiple efforts.
3. **The fastest path to success:** You will obviously reach your goal faster if you give it all you've got and not hedge your bets, but this can also be scary. Take a moment and ask yourself: Does the success I hope to attain or goal I want to achieve outweigh my fear of the commitment level necessary to get there?" This will bring you to the "Veracruz moment" of decision.

COMMITMENT

Perhaps you are faced with "Veracruz moments" right now and are unsure of what to do. Many of us may delay important decisions, put off pursuing our dreams, or avoid risk out of caution, raw fear, or some other reason. Maybe it's time to face these critical moments and abandon your escape plan. Carefully consider whether you are ready to go all in regarding a big decision in your life and be 100 percent committed.

It may be time to burn the ships.

Are you facing a big decision in your life at this time? What can you do to be "all in" with your level of commitment and move forward? Begin implementing the best practices shared here and evaluate your progress over the next ninety days.

CHAPTER 8

Contentment

What Is Success?

⁓

Let your life be free from love of money but be content with what you have, for he has said, "I will never forsake you or abandon you."
HEBREWS 13:5, NAB

My parents were always active in the lives of my two sons through their visits to see us in Atlanta, weekly phone calls, and our visits to their home in Florida. My mother passed away in 2010, and my father is fortunately still with us but rarely travels from his home in Florida anymore because of his health. We still talk weekly and visit him when we can. I am grateful that he and my mother, when she was alive, always had a close relationship with their grandchildren.

I recall one Saturday thirteen years ago after my father had just returned to Florida after a long visit. My younger son and I were throwing the football in our front yard, and I could tell he had something on his mind. I probed and asked my son if there was anything he wanted to talk about. He responded with "Dad, remember when we talked about what it means to be successful a few months ago? Were Nana and Papa successful?"

Wow! That was an interesting and mature question. He was referring to a conversation we had a few months before about being successful in business and what kind of career he wanted to have after college. I gave him a thoroughly modern version of what I thought success looked like in business and made sure we talked about having strong faith and the importance of starting and caring for a family someday as well. I kept it at a high level for him at that time, but his question about my parents deserved a deeper answer.

I explained that my mom and dad came from a different generation. My dad was in the army for six years after high school before going to work full-time. He met and married my mother, who also worked for the same company, in 1965, and I came along in 1966. We didn't have a lot of extras when I was growing up, but we had what we needed. Both my parents worked, but we always had dinner together, and my father frequently coached my sports teams. They were both active volunteers at our church and volunteered in the community where we lived. Even though my parents did not finish college, they both instilled in me a passion for learning when I was young, and there was no question in their minds that I would continue my education after high school. The same was true for my younger sister.

My parents taught us about faith, the importance of serving others, and the virtue of hard work. My sister and I knew how to be self-sufficient at a young age. Strong values and great life lessons were instilled in us from my earliest childhood memories. My parents also handled adversity in their lives with a calmness and determination that inspires me to this day. They always seemed to possess a sense of peace, no matter what the circumstances. So, were my parents successful? By modern standards, a quick glance at their meager savings and lack of material possessions would merit a resounding "no." But in the areas that mattered most to my father—and to my mother while she was alive—my parents were incredibly blessed all their lives with everything of consequence they truly desired. They were truly content, and they modeled this virtue beautifully for me and my sister.

You see, my parents never tried to "keep up with the Joneses." Acquiring toys and accumulating wealth never mattered. They were focused on raising faith-filled children, helping as much as possible with furthering our education, and teaching us how to be responsible. These days my father always wants to talk about his grandchildren or find out how my business is doing when I call him. He rarely talks about himself, and he certainly never complains.

My parents came from a generation that has much to teach us. We can deceive ourselves all we want that today's world holds us to a different standard, but as I get older, I recognize that we also have the ability to choose the lives we want to lead. The more I detach myself from modern society's view of success, the easier it is for me to practice the virtue of contentment and the more fulfilled I feel. This detachment allows me to put the appropriate focus on serving God and living my faith, loving and spending time with my wife and children, and giving back to others instead of accumulating unnecessary toys that can often become obstacles to true happiness. I learned these invaluable lessons from my parents—especially my father.

So, back to my son's question: "Are Nana and Papa successful?" As I reflect on their lives and write this chapter, I have to say that my parents were the most successful people I have ever known. I hope I can emulate their example over the course of my life.

The idea of success that many of us have been taught at a young age is often an illusion that can create frustration, anxiety, and years of wasted time as we wind up chasing things that may not be what we need or even important as we grow older. My parents were wise enough to avoid this trap, and did their best to convey the lesson to me, although I must admit I spent the early years of my career desperately trying to live up to the expectations the world placed before me.

My father, who is now in his eighties, has spent most of his life disinterested in anything other than becoming the best husband, father, grandfather, and selfless servant to others he can be. He has never chased the illusion of worldly success that drives so many others, and yet he is the happiest and most fulfilled man I know. My mother had the exact same approach to life until her death in 2009. The happy embrace of the virtue of contentment permeated every aspect of their lives.

Having clarity about why we do what we do and our goals in life are incredibly fundamental and important. Reflect on what it is you are chasing in life and carefully consider if you

CONTENTMENT

are fulfilled. *Are you content?* This is a question we all must answer for ourselves and the answer will ultimately have a tremendous ripple effect on how we live our lives.

After pondering the lessons of this chapter, how will you know if you are "successful"? Is your current definition of success truly making you happy? If not, I encourage you to work on developing a new one that draws on the lessons about the virtue of contentment from my parents that I have shared.

CHAPTER 9

Credibility

Credibility Matters

☙

Never forget that credibility can be earned or lost every day of your life, and you need to take it seriously.

MY FATHER'S ADVICE TO ME AS A YOUNG PROFESSIONAL

The virtue of *credibility* is important. It is one of the most important things a professional must possess to grow in their career and be successful. True credibility can't be bought, and nobody should feel they are entitled to it. It must be earned, and it requires self-awareness, hard work, time, and patience. Once earned, credibility cannot be taken for granted; it can be lost, damaged, or enhanced by our actions every single day. Credibility should matter to everyone, regardless of their age or station in life, but this chapter is primarily written for college students and new business professionals interested in growing their careers and making a positive mark in the business world.

One of the first things to understand about the virtue of credibility is that your perception of your own credibility is likely not always the same as the perception of those around you. Like it or not, you are being scrutinized with "silent judgment" by those who have a significant say in you getting your internship, first job, next job, or promotion at work. This is the hard truth: From the very first encounter, you are being evaluated on a host of areas that may have nothing to do with your resume, educational background, or current work experience. During interviews or networking conversations, decision-makers in the business world are gauging your likability, integrity, values, professionalism, ability to do a great job, how you will mesh with the team, how you will fit into the company culture, etc. Their willingness to help you, advocate for you, hire you, or promote you is based on the credibility you show through characteristics you exhibit in your personal and professional life. If you have perceived credibility, this reduces their risk and builds trust in your abilities.

How Do We Show Up as Credible?

I am fortunate in my professional and personal life to engage with college students and new professionals on a frequent basis. As I work with these aspiring leaders, I often share these **ten helpful and proven tips** for making a good first impression and showing up as credible:

1. **Be courteous, respectful, punctual, and grateful.** These are table stakes and fundamental. A huge part of being considered credible during a first professional encounter is showing basic courtesy,

respect, punctuality, and gratitude. Always being on time, saying *please, thank you, sir, ma'am,* and sending handwritten thank you notes after meetings are concepts that never go out of style and always enhance credibility.

2. **Be responsive.** When communicating with anyone, especially in the business world, being responsive in a timely manner is very important. I strongly encourage use of the twenty-four-hour rule in all communication responses. Waiting any longer to respond signals a lack of interest and creates a bad impression with professionals on the other end. Also, make sure all communications, especially via email, are professionally written and free of grammatical errors.

3. **Follow through.** Always, always, always do what you say you will do—and *never* make excuses. Honor your commitments. If you say you will get back to someone tomorrow, then do it. If you say you will take care of a task or assume ownership of something, then do it. Lack of follow through and excuse-making is a red alert signal that perhaps you cannot be trusted, and this negatively impacts your credibility.

4. **Be sincere and vulnerable.** True credibility comes from a place of sincerity and can't be faked. Be real and don't be afraid to show vulnerability. For example, admitting that you don't know the answer to a question or sharing that you are sometimes uncomfortable with networking can help you gain credibility with more senior leaders.

5. **Always do the right thing.** Always live with integrity. Live by your values, principles, and code of ethics in all areas of your life. Be honest and accountable for your actions in all situations. This is hopefully core to who you are, and you should never be afraid of sacrificing a little professional success for the knowledge that you consistently do the right thing. The most credible leaders I know lead with their values front and center.

6. **Cultivate a professional image.** In the age of virtual meetings, many of us have gotten a little relaxed in our dress code/image. When you are a student or new professional looking to establish yourself as credible, *go the other direction*. Always dress professionally and be well groomed. This doesn't mean you have to wear a tie or a nice dress to every encounter, but avoid jeans, T-shirts, or anything else that indicates you are less than professional. Also, make sure your resume is professionally done. Avoid sounding overly familiar at the beginning of a new professional relationship, and never use slang or inappropriate language. First impressions really do matter.

7. **Be careful with your online presence.** In today's polarized and politically charged world, be cautious about what you post online. Companies often research your online footprint, and an inappropriate meme or an angry comment can negatively impact your credibility, career growth, and even employability in a way that is easily avoidable.

8. **Tell your story well.** Every personal work experience, volunteer activity, participation on a sports team, travel experience, and college course is part of your compelling personal story, regardless of your age. This is also true of where you grew up, adversity you may have faced, and successes you have achieved. How well you weave these pieces of your story together and share them with others is a key part of being seen as credible and relatable to others.
9. **Do consistently good work.** It should go without saying that your work should speak for itself. Let your consistent hard work and excellent results do your talking for you. This is a foundational part of professional credibility, and all new professionals have the same opportunity to shine.
10. **Volunteer, but do not overcommit.** Ask for the difficult tasks and the jobs nobody else wants. Endure longer hours to finish the tough projects. Volunteering can and should also mean spending time in the community supporting great causes. All of this enhances credibility, but be careful to not overcommit yourself. Use good judgment and don't overextend yourself to the point that your day job suffers.

How Do We Seek Help with Credibility from Others?

Personal credibility is a worthy goal for all of us, but it is not a journey we have to travel alone. I have greatly benefited from the help and wise counsel of more senior leaders, friends, and family in my career who have played helpful roles as I strove to be more credible over the years. Here are **three important ways** to enlist the help of others:

1. **Ask for candid feedback.** Are you credible? Consistently go to people in your life who will be brutally honest with you. Give them permission to tell you what they really think and ask them if you come across as credible. Get their specific guidance on what you can do to improve. This courageous practice can help you grow and stay on track.
2. **Seek out mentors and advocates.** I benefited a great deal from helpful mentors early in my career who taught me through their personal examples how to authentically grow in credibility, and I will always be grateful to these amazing men and women. I also encountered advocates along the way who went to bat for me regarding new jobs, promotions, and other career opportunities. I had to earn their trust and advocacy through diligence, hard work, and results, but these key leaders made connections for me and helped open doors I might not have been able to open on my own. *Helpful tip*: When someone does something like this for you, they are taking a chance and putting their own credibility at risk. Go to great lengths to honor their kind act and never do anything to make them regret it.
3. **Build a strong network of relationships.** Your goal over time is to build a deep and diverse network of

trusted professionals and colleagues who will provide you with ongoing mentoring, advice, and candid feedback as you progress at your job and in your career. *Always seek to associate with other professionals who are credible.* The key is to work hard at getting to know as many people as you can on a more personal level. These contacts and connections can be critical mentors, sounding boards for your ideas, and potential advocates for you and your work throughout the organization. Demonstrate to them your motivation, commitment, and relevant expertise, and whenever possible, find ways you can be of service to them and help them with their work.

I wrote this chapter out of a sincere desire to help and support college students and early career professionals who may not be hearing enough of this advice in school or the workplace. What I have shared comes from three decades of experience, and I promise that these ideas and approaches work. I hope it is obvious to more senior leaders who are reading this chapter that you and I have to be mindful of our credibility as well. We can never take it for granted, and much of the advice here applies to us as well. I also hope we will actively engage with this next generation of leaders and advise them on the importance of credibility—and most importantly, *give them great role models to follow.*

After reading this chapter on the virtue of credibility, how would you rate yourself? Where can you improve? If you believe changes are needed, what specific actions can you

PRACTICAL VIRTUE

take to improve your own credibility? Who will help hold you accountable?

CHAPTER 10

Curiosity

Cultivating the Curiosity Skill Set

The greatest compliment was ever paid me was when someone asked me what I thought and attended to my answer.
Henry David Thoreau

Curiosity is one of my favorite skills and a virtue I have worked hard to develop ever since I was a new professional just out of college. I love to ask questions and learn about people's lives, interests, challenges, and successes, and I am always willing to be transparent and share about my life as well. I have long realized that when you're genuinely curious, you must actively listen to the other person. Nothing builds trust and deepens relationships more effectively than allowing another person to feel truly listened to and valued. I am also a strong advocate for getting to know both the personal and work aspects of someone's life, with a preference for the personal side first.

Forging New Relationships

An effective starting point for all relationships is building *empathy*—stepping into the other person's shoes and seeing the world through their eyes. We accomplish this by breaking down walls and building rapport through genuine curiosity. Here are some of my favorite questions when I meet someone new in both personal and work settings:

- "What sort of work do you do?"
- "Did you do anything fun this past weekend?
- "What are your plans this coming weekend?"
- "When you are not working, where do you like to invest your time and energy?"
- "This has been an interesting year filled with challenges and surprises. What are you doing to deal with everything personally and professionally?"

Notice that none of these questions will solicit simple yes or no answers; instead, they require responses that will give you helpful insights into who the person is and what is interesting and important to them. After carefully listening to their answers, you will find that you can highlight shared experiences and introduce additional questions informed by what you just learned about them:

- "That is very interesting. I used to be a runner as well. Do you run any competitive races? What else do you do to stay fit?"

- "That sounds like a great trip. My family loves to travel as well. What are some of your favorite destinations?"
- "I agree. It has been an interesting year for us as well. You mentioned job stress . . . what sort of work do you do?"

When we encounter new people, we utilize the skill of curiosity to learn more about them—to find areas of similarity or shared interests. By asking people questions, we also have an opportunity to show genuine *interest* and *respect*. We should always try to balance seeking information about them with sharing information about ourselves. A good conversation is not a one-way monologue, but rather an exchange in which two people are genuinely engaged, listening, responding, and connecting to each other. In fact, our willingness to share a little about ourselves *first* can often be a helpful way to encourage the other person to share as well in response to our questions. Recognize that authenticity is also greatly enhanced by mutual sharing—and sharing thrives in an atmosphere of curiosity. Here are two examples:

- "My wife and I had a really full weekend with the kids. With the kids' sports activities, yard projects, and church, we had a lot going on. How was your weekend?"
- "Working from home has posed some interesting challenges for me, and I am still trying to figure it out. Do you work from home? Can you share any insights with me about how to be more effective from a home office?"

Positioning the question after you share first can elicit a deeper response from the other person and encourage them to give more substantive answers. Also, this approach gives the other person complete freedom and discretion to share as much or little information as they choose. Going deeper is always better in my opinion, but not everyone is ready to share as much as you, and that is perfectly fine. Be respectful. Be patient.

The Virtue of Curiosity at Work

I observe that leaders and other professionals in my network often overlook the value of curiosity in work conversations. Curiosity at work will help you transform "work colleagues" into valuable and mutually beneficial professional relationships, as well as foster greater engagement. We are typically so busy that we may feel there isn't enough time to invest in a conversation that deviates from the business at hand. What a missed opportunity! We often fail to learn about how our colleagues are really doing, what they are feeling, and how they are experiencing life in general. We may end up getting perfunctory answers to our work questions instead of the more honest and open discussions we crave.

The answer might be more patience and better listening on our part. Perhaps we should meet our team members and colleagues where they are and invest in getting to know more about their interests and lives outside of work. We may need to simply ask their opinion with a sincere desire to hear their thoughts . . . and just absorb what they say without judgment. By the way, this investment in curiosity, listening, and discussing the personal side of life builds trust, which is also an essential building block of strong business relationships.

Curiosity to Improve Engagement and Performance

I can't think of a single business leader who would not benefit from demonstrating more curiosity at work. We often miss opportunities for candid and substantive conversations because we fail to ask questions and show genuine curiosity. Asking probing questions of others rather than merely stating our opinions can often provide an opportunity to bring difficult topics to light, drive better results with our team members, and help us improve our own performance. Examples can look like this:

- "Mike, do you feel like you are having the kind of success you hoped for in your new role?"
- "Sarah, I am concerned that you might miss your goals this quarter. What do you see as the obstacles in your way and how can I help you overcome them?"
- Here are some other examples of powerful questions:
- "I am new to my role. Do you have specific coaching tips for me on how I can be successful?"
- "Can you help me understand . . . ?"
- "What is something you are working on that you are excited about?"
- "I don't think I did a very good job presenting yesterday. Do you have specific tips on how I can improve my content and presenting style?"

- "What are at least three obstacles holding us back from the success we want?"
- "What are we doing right now as a team that is working well?"
- "What do you need most from me right now?"

It should go without saying that there are obligations associated with these kinds of questions. We have a responsibility to help people feel psychologically safe and comfortable in sharing what they really think. We have an obligation to actively listen and demonstrate that we've clearly heard them. We have a responsibility to follow up, explore further, and hold them and ourselves accountable to any specific commitments made in these conversations. If curiosity is going to thrive and we desire to grow this skill, we have to practice it and follow through when we utilize it.

Curiosity to Strengthen Personal Connection at Work

Take the time to invest in meeting people where they are. Be patient, as it may take a while for them to trust you and feel comfortable opening up. Be intentional about scheduling one-on-one conversations with colleagues where work is only a sliver of the agenda and the rest is good old-fashioned conversation filled with life, family, struggles, successes, and hopefully a little humor. Ask questions with an authentic desire to learn about the other person. Three of my favorite questions I use with coaching clients at the beginning of a conversation are:

- "Can we talk about life outside of work for a few minutes before we jump into business?"
- "How is life treating you?"
- "How is your family?"

Show sincere interest. Actively listen. Take notes to demonstrate the importance of what is being discussed. Be empathetic.

Commit to being insatiably curious about others. Learn and remember personal things about others such as their spouse and kids' names, hobbies, interests, and birthdays. Remember that people find you more interesting when you ask questions. Stuck on knowing the perfect thing to say? *Ask questions.* Want to make a favorable impression on a colleague, key stakeholder, manager, or others in your network and learn important information about them? *Ask questions.* Want to transform your work acquaintances into solid relationships? *Ask questions.*

Six Best Practices for Fostering the Virtue of Curiosity

I am a keen observer of people and am always interested in gathering best practices for personal and professional growth I can use and share with others. It is my belief that curiosity is a competency and a virtue that can be cultivated and developed like any other. As I reflect on people in my network who excel at curiosity, these are the behaviors and mindsets I believe they consistently exhibit to foster this valuable skill:

1. **It's not all about me:** People who are great at curiosity understand that we can't focus only on our own agendas, needs, and interests. They recognize what a turnoff it is for others when we make the conversation all about us, and instead they always strive for truly two-way conversations.
2. **Willingness to learn:** Genuinely curious people have a strong desire to learn and ask questions to enrich their understanding, acquire knowledge, and grow. We model curiosity for those around us when we show a willingness to ask questions and humbly admit we don't always know the answer.
3. **No need to be in control:** Effective curiosity is about being comfortable with the unknown. It's OK to not know how the conversation will turn out and take a leap of faith that it will unfold as it should without micromanaging or forcing our preferred outcome.
4. **Understanding the danger of certainty:** Certainty is when we are convinced that our opinions are definitely true and may be rooted to some degree in ego or arrogance. This can lead to incorrect assumptions about others and having a closed mind when engaging in conversation. It can also lead us to choke off dialogue by trying to solve every problem because we are convinced we have the answers. Curiosity is often an effective antidote to certainty.
5. **It's a human thing:** We humans desire connection and relationship, even if we would describe ourselves as having shy or introverted personalities. Curiosity

provides the catalyst for transforming boring or one-sided conversations into opportunities for greater engagement and hopefully stronger relationships.
6. **Promoting psychological safety:** People who are the most effective practitioners of curiosity are excellent at making people feel safe and comfortable (with zero repercussions) about honestly speaking their minds, sharing ideas, pointing out problems, and sharing personal aspects of their lives (even their personal struggles).

I have learned from my parents, mentors, and other leaders I have worked with over the course of my career that curiosity is an invaluable skill we all can and should more fully develop. Embracing the virtue of curiosity is the essential catalyst for building relationships, increasing engagement with colleagues, and improving our performance as well as the performance of our work colleagues. It helps us learn and enrich our lives by inviting others to share their wisdom with us. Reflect on this final thought: The next time you are in a conversation with anyone, remember that we would all be better served to do less telling and *more asking*.

How curious are you? How will you grow your curiosity skills based on what you learned in this chapter, beginning tomorrow? Will you commit to making the virtue of curiosity your new superpower?

CHAPTER 11

Generosity

Thoughtfully Considering the Power of Generosity

˞

It is every man's obligation to put back into the world at least the equivalent of what he takes out of it.

ALBERT EINSTEIN

G*enerosity* is one of my favorite words and a virtue I greatly admire in others. I would like to share some thoughts with you on generosity that will encourage you to pause and reflect, but also hopefully influence how you live now and the rest of your life. Would you agree that generosity inspires gratitude, and gratitude inspires generosity? Let me share a brief story that illustrates this point.

An admirer of the great German composer Johannes Brahms left him a large sum of money in his will. When he learned of the generous gift, the composer was reported to be deeply moved. Instead of keeping the generous gift from his benefactor, he declared he did not need the money and gave it to those more in need.

The generosity shown to Brahms was immediately passed along by the composer to those in need. The virtue of generosity that affected Brahms inspired duplication of itself in the generosity Brahms himself demonstrated to others. We would also hope that it stirred the same virtue among the beneficiaries of his gifts. When we consider that there is a *ripple effect* resulting from our generosity, we may be compelled to be more thoughtful and focused on giving to those we engage with each day. If we reflect more deeply on this, it is clear that generosity is the virtue that can go on duplicating itself forever.

The greatest gift we can give to someone is the gift of ourselves. Giving of ourselves is the perfect practice of the virtue of generosity. The impulse toward generosity is implanted in the depth of man's very being from our creation. Consequently, to live a truly authentic and meaningful life means to give generously to others. For those of us who are Christians, we know God's gift of Himself through His son, Jesus Christ, represents the highest form of generosity and serves as a shining example for the practice of generosity by all mankind. We are reminded of this tremendous gift to the world every year in the celebration of Christmas.

As a virtue, does generosity have limits? Since virtue is rooted in love, this question is similar to us asking, "Does love have limits?" If we indulge the analytical side of our brains, being generous seems to cost us something and perhaps feel uncomfortable at times. If we live with a generous heart, acting from a place of greed seems almost beyond understanding. It is acting with greed that makes us poorer, not generosity. True generosity, when practiced consistently and well, enriches our lives beyond measure. I believe there is an abundance of generosity within each of us, waiting to come out. Not to release it is to cost us a piece of who we are. Nothing is more expensive and demanding than greed. Nothing is more satisfying and ultimately good for us than generosity.

If we consider famous characters such as Ebenezer Scrooge and The Grinch, we will realize they were driven by their greediness in such a way that the greedier they become, the less human they appear to us. The eventual conversions of Scrooge and The Grinch are actually returns to humanity that are joyfully appreciated by the reader. People living lives firmly rooted in generosity are not only more likable than those who are greedy, but they also appear to be more human and certainly more authentic. Do you agree?

Winston Churchill said, "We make a living by what we get. We make a life by what we give." It is obviously more blessed to give than to receive, and it is certainly far more blessed to give than to take. For a moment, let's thoughtfully consider how the gift of our time, our willingness to listen, our patience, our mercy, our talents, our kindness, our love, and our financial resources can be applied to more intentionally living the virtue of generosity toward others. In the end, we cannot take with us what we have, though many of us seem to live as though we could. But we can joyfully share what we have been given, accumulated, or earned with the people we encounter each day. Finally, remember that generosity is a virtue for everyone—not only for the prosperous and blessed. Generosity can take many forms, and everyone has an opportunity to enjoy the fruits of this virtue, regardless of their struggles or situation in life.

Who will benefit from your generosity today?

I encourage you to be more intentional about practicing the virtue of generosity in the days ahead. Think about how to improve this practice at work, with family, with friends, and in your community. A great way to grow in generosity is to quietly think at the beginning of every encounter, How can I best serve and help this person? *and see the goodness that follows.*

CHAPTER 12

Gratitude

Live Life Gratefully

☙

When it comes to life, the critical thing is whether you take things for granted or take them with gratitude.
G. K. CHESTERTON, FROM HIS AUTOBIOGRAPHY, 1936

At a very young age, my parents constantly urged me to always say thank you in response to any kindness or friendly words shared in my direction. For many years, I saw this advice from my parents as simply good manners and what people were supposed to do. In my mid-teen years, I was mature enough to observe the heartfelt sincerity my parents always showed when they said thank you to others, offered prayers of thanks, or expressed appreciation for the simple blessings in their lives—and how different this was from my perfunctory use of the words. They really meant it, and I began to understand that their use of the words thank you transcended mere courtesy and clearly meant something much more meaningful and powerful to them. What I observed my parents practicing so well was the beginning of my deeper understanding of the virtue of *gratitude*.

My parents were wonderful role models and teachers in many ways, and helping me learn to be grateful was an amazing gift that I work at demonstrating every day. My wife and I try very hard to model a life of gratefulness for our sons and for those we encounter each day, and this ongoing effort has absolutely transformed us.

What Are Some of the Fruits of Gratitude?

- We desire less when we are truly grateful for what we already have in our lives.
- People who are grateful for what they have are more generous to those in need.
- Gratitude requires a positive frame of mind, which contributes to greater overall happiness. There cannot be happiness without gratitude.
- Consistently practicing gratitude with others results in a ripple effect; those experiencing our gratitude pay it forward to the people they encounter.
- We positively impact and grow our relationships with a grateful attitude.
- Gratitude is a healthy substitute for resentment, envy, jealousy, and greed (see point number one).

Many people, often myself included, find it challenging to consistently act with gratitude. The great writer G. K. Chesterton observed: "Gratitude, being nearly the greatest of human duties, is also nearly the most difficult."

What are best practices we can follow to help us be more grateful?

Six Gratitude Best Practices

1. **Learn to be grateful for your challenges, not just your blessings.** Look at adversity as a source of helpful lessons rather than frustrating burdens to carry.
2. **Express gratitude at every opportunity.** "I am grateful," "I appreciate," and a simple "Thank you" can never be overused and should be shared throughout the day when an appropriate opportunity arises.
3. **Make it memorable.** Send a handwritten note of gratitude whenever possible.
4. **Be intentional.** Place a reminder on the calendar each Friday morning to express gratitude for the people and blessings you have experienced during the week.
5. **Be grateful for EVERYTHING.** "Cultivate the habit of being grateful for every good thing that comes to you, and to give thanks continuously. And because all things have contributed to your advancement, you should include all things in your gratitude" (Ralph Waldo Emerson).
6. **Always give thanks to God.** Be grateful to God for the gift of your life, for air in your lungs, the shining sun on your face, and for all Creation. Share this gratitude in prayer throughout the day. "God's generous presence in our lives lays claim to a form of gratitude that is never satisfied by the mere recitation of thanks but requires us to express our gratitude in action. The

kind of gratitude that God is hoping to find is one that includes a bond of friendship and a commitment to service" (Donald DeMarco, *The Many Faces of Virtue*).

As you consider how to go about living your life and interacting with those you encounter each day, why not choose to embrace the virtue of gratitude? Make the commitment and watch your life absolutely change for the better.

Live gratefully and you will *never* regret it.

At the end of each day this month, write down three things you are grateful for and at least two specific ways you have practiced the virtue of gratitude. Consider extending the practice if you find value in it and encourage others to do the same.

CHAPTER 13

Hard Work

What It Takes to Make the Most of Opportunity

༄

Success in business requires training and discipline and hard work. But if you're not frightened by these things, the opportunities are just as great today as they ever were.
DAVID ROCKEFELLER, former chairman and CEO of
Chase Manhattan Corporation

I was speaking with a senior executive friend recently about the challenges of attracting, motivating, and retaining talent in her company. She described at great length the generous benefits and perks offered by her organization to future and current employees—it actually was a bit overwhelming to consider all someone would receive if they currently worked for or joined her company. This conversation was similar to others I've had with various senior leaders, and it reminds me that the war for talent has been raging for years. It is understandable that companies are increasingly getting more creative and aggressive in trying to attract and keep good people, but I believe we may be overlooking the most important benefit and perk of all: We should be talking more about opportunity and the virtue it requires to make the most of it: *hard work.*

What I'm about to share is a bit countercultural and will possibly make some of you uncomfortable. I know there are exceptions, but it seems as if corporate America has been engaging in an unsustainable contest for several years now to outdo one another with ever more generous benefits and perks for future and current employees that is spiraling out of control. The current uncertain trajectory of the economy and increasing corporate layoffs will likely force companies to rein in benefits and perks somewhat, but the essential problem of how we think about attracting, motivating, and retaining talent will remain.

What Are the Consequences?

This way of thinking contributes to an entitlement culture that certainly exists beyond the workplace, where the more we give, the more people expect—with no end in sight. This entitlement mentality can sometimes lead to a lack of appreciation from employees for what is being given to them or done for them. It can contribute to thinking, *You are lucky to have me* instead of *I am lucky to be here*. I am suggesting that we have over-indexed on this so much that we may have forgotten the importance of simply discussing and selling opportunities and the virtue of hard work:

You will earn, learn, achieve, attain . . . *if* you work hard, perform well, make a commitment, and so on. For example, we are offering:

- The **opportunity** to be compensated well for producing consistent results
- The **opportunity** to potentially earn stock with performance and tenure
- The **opportunity** to move up quickly based on attitude, hard work, and performance
- The **opportunity** to be developed, mentored, and grown by leaders and the company
- The **opportunity** to create, support, or sell products or services that will make a positive difference in the world
- The **opportunity** to be part of something special and help build a world-class organization

Of course, today's talent landscape may require us to offer competitive salaries, aggressive bonuses, and attractive healthcare or PTO plans, but those are table stakes and follow the demands of the marketplace and the whims of the economy. If we better promote the idea of opportunities and what it will take to achieve those opportunities, we will likely attract a higher-caliber candidate who is self-motivated, hardworking, and driven to succeed . . . a candidate who is willing to work hard and eager to learn and grow. This type of candidate will be grateful for the benefits and perks, but even more grateful for the clear opportunity to excel and prove themselves. Overall, this candidate will likely be more appreciative of the opportunities placed in front of them and more likely to be a long-term member of the team if the company honors its commitments.

I am reminded of my first three corporate jobs in the first twenty-five years of my career before I launched my executive coaching company in 2012. My first job out of college as a manager trainee with a national retailer promised me excellent training, fast career growth, and a solid income opportunity if I worked hard and showed initiative. I made the most of this opportunity and grew to a senior operational leadership role.

My second job as a director of recruiting with a national restaurant chain began with this promise in the interview from my future boss: "This will be the toughest job you have ever had, but you will have the opportunity to learn more here about people, leadership, and business than any job you will ever have and grow in ways you never thought possible." And it truly was the toughest job I ever had and stretched me in often uncomfortable ways, but I am grateful for all that I learned before leaving after four years as a vice-president and an officer of the company.

My final corporate role was with a national executive search firm that hired me as managing partner. The opportunity this firm offered was quite different. I would have the opportunity to earn an uncapped income based on performance, work with well-respected servant leaders who led the firm, and make a positive difference in the lives of our clients, candidates, and the community. All of this was true (and more) when I left as a partner and shareholder of this wonderful organization thirteen years later to start my own coaching and leadership development company.

I look back over my career with great appreciation for all the opportunities I have been given and the chances to prove myself and achieve the career success I have been blessed to experience. *Each of these opportunities represents an example to follow for professionals today.* In each of my roles, I was only promised an *opportunity* if I was committed, embraced the virtue of hard work, and produced results. I made the most of it—and the virtue that served me best was the virtue of hard work.

If you are an early career professional, reflect carefully on your current job and the opportunities in front of you. *Do you feel stuck?* If you look in the mirror, the only thing that may holding you back is . . . you. You are smart, talented, and absolutely have the ability to make the most of where you are at this stage of your career journey. I am confident you are working hard, but I encourage you to embrace working even harder, putting in longer hours if needed, raising your hand for difficult assignments, and recognizing that opportunities are usually earned, not given. Seek clarity from your boss on their expectations and advice on what it takes to make the most of your opportunities and consistently ask for candid feedback at appropriate times to determine if you are exceeding those expectations.

Reflect on your experiences at this stage of your career. How are you viewing opportunity and how to make the most of it? If what you are doing is not achieving the desired results, consider embracing one of the few things over which you have 100 percent control: the virtue of hard work. Commit to this path and evaluate your results in six months with the help of your boss and accountability partners.

CHAPTER 14

Humility

A Man I Know

↣

The three most important virtues are humility, humility, and humility.
St. Bernard of Clairvaux

I lit a candle and prayed in our parish chapel not long ago for a man I know in his mid-eighties who is struggling with various health issues. The candle I lit burned brightly, more brightly than the others, for the hour I was in the chapel. The light reminded me of this man's life, which was filled with countless good examples and a wonderful legacy of the lives he has touched. Let me tell you a little about him.

He had a challenging childhood. His father left when he was a little boy, and he, his two brothers, and his twin sister were raised by his alcoholic mother and grandmother. He made his way through childhood with no real fatherly influence and very little money to keep the household going. He was good at sports and played high school football; he focused on girls and going to the beach as ways to escape the emotional turmoil at home.

He joined the Army at age eighteen, and the military formed the basis for the man he became. He learned self-discipline, gained a work ethic, and became a leader. After six years, he left to join the real world and start his career. He was very different from the rash teenager he had been; he was now a mature and humble man focused on starting a new life. He met and fell in love with a woman a few years later, and they settled down to start a family.

The happy couple had a boy, and both parents got busy pursuing their careers and raising their child. The man tried college, but after two years decided it was not for him and focused instead on working as hard as he could to support his family. The man created the opposite of his own childhood experience. Although he was not perfect, he always made time after work to play catch with his son and teach him valuable life lessons. He loved talking to his son about the importance of getting a good education, working hard, helping others in need, and always doing your best. This hardworking father grew up in a generation that didn't easily show affection, and he was rarely heard to say, "I love you," but his actions showed the depth of his feelings toward his family more than words ever could.

A daughter was born after the man and his wife moved to Georgia in the early 1970s, and now the family was complete. The years went by, and the man started attending church at the urging of his wife. He found a true calling as a Sunday School teacher and faithful member of his church. The man and woman continued to raise their children. They built a good moral foundation in the home and set great examples with their humility, work ethic, service to others and devotion to family. The man was well known in the community as a good friend, hard worker, humble, a selfless giver, great father, and devoted husband.

He saw first his son off to college, and years later, his daughter. He had always placed a premium on education, and it made him very proud to see his children live out his dream. Disappointments and triumphs followed in the next several years as the man watched his children stumble, fall, and get back up again in their own pursuit of life, love, and happiness. He just kept on working and humbly giving testimony with his life; his children could easily see a great example to follow, even if they didn't always appreciate him.

The later years saw the son raise a family of his own and the daughter get married, have a son, and get divorced. Out of his sense of duty and compassion, he and his wife took their daughter and her child into their home, and they helped to raise their grandson. The man still taught the timeless lessons of faith, having a good work ethic, strong values, and the value of education. His happiest moments always seemed to be a teaching opportunity with his daughter's son and the sons of his firstborn.

Today, the man's age, a lifetime of hard work, and various health challenges have caught up with him. Even when he is not feeling well, though, he always smiles and makes the conversation about you, not him. For this man, his humble focus has always been about serving others, not himself. In a world that often celebrates self-promotion and self-importance, his lifelong practice of the virtue of humility shines as a beacon of light and grace.

I wonder if he recognizes how many lives he has touched by the example of his incredible work ethic, making good moral choices, and always offering to give of himself to others—never asking for anything in return. He was married to the same woman for forty-five years until her death in February 2010, and the dignified, humble and caring way he handled her loss was another grace-filled example to emulate. I hope he knows how he has influenced me by the meaningful life he has led.

The man is known by several names: husband, brother, friend, Papa, and Steve. I have always just called him . . . Dad.

Dad, thank you for being the best example a son could ever want and for showing me how to pursue and live a meaningful life guided by the virtue of humility and a passion for serving others. I hope I pass along what you have taught me to my own children.

How does this story speak to you? What can you glean from this man's focus on a humble life always lived in the service of others? How are you doing with practicing this powerful virtue? What steps can you take to activate and grow the virtue of humility in your life?

CHAPTER 15

Joy

The Attractiveness of Joy

There can be no joy in living without joy in work.
ST. THOMAS AQUINAS

I recently spoke with a senior leader in my business network on the topic of inspiring and encouraging employees after what has been a very challenging few years. As we shared observations, we were both struck by how gloomy, cynical, and anxious many leaders (and their team members) in our extended networks seem to be about life, work, and what lies ahead. This is certainly understandable in light of what we have experienced with the tough economy, overwhelming negativity from news channels and social media, the overall division in society, and a host of other challenges that are slowly wearing us down.

If you will indulge me, I would like to offer a nonscientific antidote for any of us who are feeling jaded. I know it is effective because I have seen it in action over most of my adult life. I strongly believe the best way to counter feeling jaded is to work at sincerely embracing the virtue of joy and having a more joyful mindset. I hope we can agree that jaded leaders likely struggle to inspire and encourage others, but joyful leaders excel at it. For some leaders who embrace this *joyful mindset*, the change will be like flipping a switch. For others, it may require significant effort. Regardless, I promise the journey is worth it!

How exactly do we become more joyful leaders? I could ask this question of ten different people and get ten different answers. Perhaps it would help if I describe how I observe these leaders showing up to me and others. The most effective leaders I know act differently and embrace a joy-filled approach to work and life in general. There are consistent behaviors that form the foundation of a joyful mindset in these leaders—here are some examples:

- The joyful leaders I know are **grateful** for what they have and are not focused on what they may be missing.
- They are humble and strive to give others the credit for their successes.
- They are **authentic** and consistently true to who they are at all times, regardless of the audience.
- They handle adversity with calmness, **humor**, and a focus on **learning** from difficult moments.
- They are generous with their time and invest cheerfully and selflessly in their relationships with work colleagues, friends, and family.
- They **give back** to their community and serve and support great causes.

- They are **realistic** about challenges; they don't ignore them but rather choose to be **optimistic** and **hopeful** about solving them.
- They **practice self-care** and are intentional about taking care of their physical, emotional, spiritual, and mental needs. They understand that we cannot share with others from an empty cup.
- The most joyful leaders I know have strong **faith** and recognize that their joy ultimately comes from God.

One other common behavior of the joyful leaders I know is how they consistently inspire and make others feel better, especially their work colleagues. I am reminded of this powerful quote attributed to St. Teresa of Calcutta (Mother Teresa): "Let anyone who comes to you go away feeling better and happier. Everyone should see goodness in your face, in your eyes, in your smile. Joy shows from the eyes. It appears when we speak and walk. It cannot be kept closed inside us. It reacts outside. Joy is very infectious."

As we ponder this idea of being jaded or joyful, think about the role we can play in preparing for a more positive, hopeful, and joyful future. We can fight the widespread gloom that surrounds us by spreading goodwill and the virtue of joy in our daily interactions with others. We can greet others with kindness and a smile and serve their needs as best we can. We can speak with work colleagues, friends, and family with the desire to bring joy and cheerfulness to the conversation rather than complaints or negativity. We can go out of our way to help and serve those who may be struggling in our companies, families, and communities. Wouldn't you agree that when we offer encouragement and joy to others, we are quietly fueling growth in these critical areas for ourselves as well?

Maybe all of these noble efforts can help us provide the inspiration and encouragement our work colleagues (and others) need from us right now. Maybe we will embrace this thinking because we recognize that we are beyond ready to abandon our jaded mindset and need this simple reminder. Whatever the reason, let's all do our part to create a ripple effect of joy in our spheres of influence and embrace the words of Mother Teresa above to make joy "infectious."

If we embrace the virtue of joy and sincerely practice it, others will follow. Only good things will result when we do.

Reflect for a few minutes on your current mindset. Are you feeling jaded or joyful? Depending on your state of joy, commit to modeling and improving your practice of the key behaviors of joyful leaders mentioned in this chapter. Discuss your efforts with a friend or two and encourage one another's efforts to grow in this area

CHAPTER 16

Kindness

The Importance of RAPKG

≈

The ultimate test of your greatness is the way you treat every human being.
St. John Paul II

Some time ago I received a thank you note from someone who had attended one of my corporate workshops on how to maximize business relationships. The person was thoughtful in sending the note, but I especially appreciated the specific reference to the best practices that resonated with her and how she planned to apply them in her life. This note of gratitude with the lessons it contained stuck with me and has been the catalyst for some deeper thinking about the importance of something the workplace and the world desperately need: random acts of praise, kindness and gratitude—or RAPKG for short. Although we will discuss praise, gratitude, and kindness in this chapter, praise and gratitude simply support the overarching theme and importance of the virtue of *kindness* in how we interact with others.

I have long observed that despite the myriad ways we are connected (in a superficial way) to one another through technology and social media, the opportunities for genuine and more substantive relationships are diminishing. It may be that our interest in building stronger relationships is fading as well. It is important that we fight this growing cultural norm, and RAPKG is a helpful way to do it. Consider the numerous opportunities we have each day to reach out to our work colleagues, clients, or extended network of friends and offer a brief message of praise for a job well done, do something kind for them, or express our gratitude for something they may have done for us. This approach costs us nothing and will help us strengthen old relationships and foster new ones. It is a worthwhile and noble practice we should all follow.

Getting Started

In order for RAPKG to thrive, we need to be *intentional*, *selfless*, *measured*, and *specific*. First, I recommend incorporating some *intentionality* into your "randomness" and put RAPKG on your calendar every Monday morning. Let this serve as a reminder to reflect on the people you encountered the previous week that you might want to reach out to with a note, call, email, or meeting request to offer praise, kindness, or gratitude. I do this weekly, and it takes less than thirty minutes. *Helpful tip*: If you feel compelled to act in the moment or want to practice RAPKG sooner, don't wait for Mondays!

Second, be *selfless*; don't attach expectations to your RAPKG. Make it about others, not about you. This practice is about giving to others, so don't ever keep score. You will reap rewards down the road in unexpected and delightful ways if you look at RAPKG like dropping a pebble in a pond. The ripple effect of your selfless acts will have a positive impact on the recipient and possibly others as they begin the practice toward people in their extended circles.

Third, be *measured* in how you practice RAPKG, especially in the area of praise. Unrestrained praise given too frequently has the effect of negating the positive impact intended. If everything is praise-worthy, then nothing is praise-worthy. A measured approach to praise, when it is truly deserved, is always best. Acting in a measured way is less important for sharing kindness and gratitude; my only advice is to start small and expand your efforts gradually as you begin to cultivate this practice in your daily life. This will help you feel less overwhelmed by the daily opportunities to practice RAPKG.

Finally, be *specific* in your application of RAPKG. Don't reach out and say, "Hey, I just wanted you to know I think you are awesome!" Though well intended, you will miss an opportunity with this vague message to specifically praise a behavior or action you want to encourage more of in the other person. If someone does something for which you are grateful, tell him or her exactly what it was that inspired our gratitude. Helpful tip: Specificity is not as strictly applied to our random practice of the virtue of kindness, as ALL acts of kindness, no matter how small, are good. Remember that an act of kindness can also consist of candid and challenging feedback delivered in a respectful manner to a colleague or friend.

Ways to Apply RAPKG

In the weeks leading up to this book's publication, I took the time to document a few opportunities I had to apply RAPKG, which I hope will inspire creative ways for you to make this practice work in your own lives:

- I sent a note to one of my coaching clients praising her for the excellent leadership I observed in her during a meeting she led for her entire organization. She did an outstanding job that I wanted to acknowledge, and I also let her know I shared the positive feedback with her boss. *Helpful tip*: Always keep thank you notes on hand. They are a great way to apply RAPKG and are more meaningful than emails.
- I took time out of a particularly hectic day to have a long conversation with a security guard who works for one of my corporate clients. He told me about his upcoming weekend plans, and I asked how his family was doing. He is one of the nicest and friendliest people I have ever met. He always greets people with a smile, and I am grateful to know him. How often do we stop and invest in a conversation with the countless people from all stations in life we encounter? How often do we treat them as they deserve with courtesy, respect, and kindness? "Kind words can be short and easy to speak, but their echoes are truly endless" (Saint Teresa of Calcutta).

- I had an opportunity to express gratitude to my wife for a difficult conversation she had with one of our sons. She handled it beautifully and got our son back on track. My wife was not aware I overheard the conversation, but it meant a lot to her that I recognized the difficulty and thanked her.

More Examples of RAPKG

- A senior executive sent flowers and a thank-you note to the wife of one of his direct reports to express his gratitude for how she supported and encouraged her husband during an extremely difficult period for the company.
- A newly hired team member was forced to stand in for her sick boss and give a nerve-racking and difficult presentation to the senior executive team on her tenth day with the company. She received a handwritten note from the CEO that afternoon praising her effort and offering suggestions for ways to make it even better. The CEO also offered to mentor the new team member once a month and help her acclimate to the company.
- A consultant friend of mine started the practice of making donations to the favorite causes of her clients in their name at Christmas and for other special occasions (an idea I have borrowed!). Instead of the usual fruit or cookie baskets, she demonstrates her understanding of what truly matters to her clients with her kind and thoughtful gifts in their name.

Other Ideas

- Invest time in someone who is looking for a job and offer advice and access to your network.
- Give the gift of a book that had a positive effect on you to someone who would also benefit from reading it.
- Treat your team to lunch and thank them for their hard work after a difficult project.
- Offer the gift of mentorship and advice to a new colleague and invest in their success.
- Reach out to a colleague who is experiencing difficulties outside of work and offer encouragement and a listening ear.
- Practicing gratitude leads to happiness. "I don't have to chase extraordinary moments to find happiness—it's right in front of me if I'm paying attention and practicing gratitude" (Brené Brown).

I would love to tell you that I have RAPKG all figured out, but I do not. I likely miss a significant number of opportunities each week to practice it and activate the virtue of kindness, but I am sincerely trying to improve, and I feel that I am making progress. Any effort in this area has a positive impact on others and contributes to my personal and professional growth—and that makes RAPKG even more worthwhile.

The Fruits of RAPKG

The pay-it-forward ripple effect of practicing RAPKG is

obvious, but there are other fruits to be had from putting this into practice. Here are a few:

- **Improves the quality of your relationships.** If you are interested in finding meaningful ways to actively engage with your business network outside of the usual agenda, this is an excellent option. The quality of these relationships will grow as a result of your thoughtful outreach. RAPKG removes barriers and fosters trust. Try to see kindness as the glue that binds together all quality and meaningful relationships.
- **Allows you to join the ranks of the exceptional.** The men and women I have encountered over the years who actively and quietly engage in RAPKG are often recognized as exceptional leaders within their organizations.
- **Overcomes division.** Much of the division and animosity in our society often spills over into the workplace, forcing us into cliques or silos. Practicing random acts of praise, kindness, and gratitude, if done well, transcends division and is indifferent to political affiliation, race, religious preferences, titles, sexual orientation, or socioeconomic backgrounds.

RAPKG is not another company program or "flavor of the month" concept. This is about reaching out in a positive way with a different mindset to the people we encounter every day in work and life. It's about consistently practicing the virtue of kindness toward everyone. We control this mindset, and there are no barriers or limits except the ones we create for ourselves. In addition to the numerous reasons I have shared about why RAPKG is important, it is simply the right thing to do. The workplace and the world could be transformed through more random acts of praise, kindness, and gratitude if you and I have the courage to positively change how we engage with those around us.

Is your mindset focused on being more kind? How can you more consistently embrace this virtue as well as being more grateful and praising of others? Who will be the beneficiary of your RAPKG today?

CHAPTER 17

Learning

The Journey from Learning Jobs to
Doing Work We Love

༄

Every opportunity I got, I took it as a learning experience.
SATYA NADELLA, CHAIRMAN AND CEO OF MICROSOFT

I had a conversation with an early career professional not long ago who was several months into his first post-college job. He was eager to grow his career and get started doing work he loves, but he struggled to articulate what he thought success looked like or clearly define "work he loves." He described feeling bored, disengaged, and trapped in his current job and was thinking about starting a job search, even though he was working for a Fortune 500 company that recruited him out of college, and he was doing work directly related to his degree. When he expressed an interest in the work I do, this led to a discussion about the difference between *learning jobs* and *doing work we love*.

I shared my own professional journey with him, and he

was surprised to hear about the eclectic path my career took over the years to help me learn what I was passionate about and how it prepared me to engage in the work I do today. As I mentioned in chapter 13, after graduating from college, I started out as a management trainee for a large retailer and learned how to run a business, engage with customers, and lead others as I progressed to more senior roles. I developed an interest in talent and recruiting while I was with the company and then transitioned to a large national restaurant chain, where I eventually became a senior executive leading recruiting, training, and diversity for the organization in my late twenties and early thirties. After four years, I was recruited to join and eventually lead a national executive search firm; there I developed a passion for coaching, leadership development, and writing. In my mid-forties, after a dozen years with this great firm, I decided to launch my own company so I could focus exclusively on the coaching and leadership development work I loved . . . and indulge my passion for writing. Along the way, I was blessed with great mentors and advocates who helped me and gave me wise counsel.

Why Does All This Matter?

Each of the jobs I had until I started my own company was a *learning job*, and I am truly grateful for every growth opportunity, challenge, and lesson I experienced on the way to figuring out what I was passionate about and loved doing. I embraced the virtue of learning as it applied to my career experiences, and it accelerated my growth. The first twenty-five years of my career prepared me in multiple ways to better serve the clients I love working with today. As I shared with this young professional, how can we truly know what we love doing unless we experiment and explore different career experiences to see what fits? To be clear, I thoroughly enjoyed aspects of every work experience I had before I started my business. But as time went on and I acquired new experiences, maturity, and hopefully a little wisdom, I began to better understand that I was being drawn to the work of coaching and guiding other leaders that I am so grateful to do today.

I could tell that our conversation was both enlightening and frustrating for this bright and talented future leader as he took it all in. He said he understood that it might take time, but still felt a degree of impatience that he might have to wait years to figure out what he loved to do. I gave him the following six ideas on how he might begin to both discern his calling and also maximize the learning experiences in his current job:

1. **Make a list of your skills.** What are you already good at? Also, what skills do you want to learn?
2. **Maximize your current role.** Are you pushing and stretching yourself? Are you fully executing your job and giving it 100 percent? Have you considered that doing well in the job you have versus chasing the job you don't have may be the wisest course of action?
3. **Ask your boss for help in creating a personal development plan.** Express your desire to grow, and be intentional with your supervisor about discussing what you want to get out of your career. Get his or

her input on what you can do to make this happen. How do you best utilize your skills and acquire new ones from your earlier list? Ask your supervisor and others to hold you accountable for making progress. Are there high-potential programs or other leadership development opportunities in your company you can be considered for when you qualify? Would outside leadership courses or an MBA be appropriate?

4. **Cultivate mentors and advocates.** Whom do you admire in your professional and personal circles who can teach you and help you grow? Who will give you candid feedback on how you are doing and what you need to work on? Who is willing to advocate for you and your career when you are not in the room? *Helpful tip*: Mentor and advocate relationships are special and should be treated with professionalism and care. The people who agree to invest in you are giving generously of their time, and they should always feel your gratitude and appreciation.

5. **Always be willing to reflect in real time on your ongoing experiences and learnings.** Did you enjoy the project you just completed—and if so, why? What clicks with you? What excites you? What inspires you and makes you happy? As you gain more work experience, the picture of where you want to go will likely emerge and be clearer if you take the time to reflect on what is going around you, consider how it affects you, and savor what it is teaching you. Also, don't forget to consider how you are helping others and

contributing to their success as part of your journey. I know without a doubt that this intentional reflection mindset helped me—and it's a lesson I learned from a wonderful mentor I had at my first job.

6. **Be patient and take stock at the end of every year.** You may not have to wait twenty-five years as I did to discern and engage in your dream work. At the end of every year, ask yourself if you have grown. What did you learn over the last twelve months? What new skills and experiences did you acquire? Are you challenged and learning new things? Did you get closer to understanding what you are called to do? Is the dream job or work becoming clearer in your mind? Is it time to pursue it?

Finally, be open to the influence of life, love, faith, and family. As you carefully plan this exciting career journey, be mindful that life may throw you a few curveballs. For example, you may fall in love, get married, and have a family. In my experience, the adversities I have faced, my faith, my marriage, and my children have been crucial in shaping my journey to the fulfilling career I am blessed to enjoy today.

My new acquaintance has plenty to think about, but I know he will find his way forward, and I plan to stay connected and help him any way I can. To his credit, he encouraged me to share the conversation you have read about in this chapter. I have had plenty of experience with the virtue of *learning* and *learning jobs*, and I am grateful for all the hard work I put in and every experience that shaped and prepared me for what

I do today. Now I embrace and live by the famous quote attributed to Mark Twain: "Find a job you enjoy doing, and you will never have to work a day in your life."

By the way, I may be doing work I love, but I still learn something new every day, and for that I am very grateful.

What has been your experience with learning jobs? Reflect on all of your work experiences and consider how they have shaped you into the professional you are today. Are you doing work you love? If not, how close are you to that goal? What new experiences do you need? What changes do you need to make to bring this to reality?

CHAPTER 18

Mentorship

Mentoring the Next Generation

While I made my living as a coach, I have lived my life to be a mentor-and to be mentored! . . . constantly. Everything in the world has been passed down. Every piece of knowledge is something that has been shared by someone else. If you understand it as I do, mentoring becomes your true legacy. It is the greatest inheritance you can give to others. It is why you get up every day—to teach and be taught.

JOHN WOODEN, *A GAME PLAN FOR LIFE*

Not long ago, over the span of a few weeks I encountered four young adults ranging in age from nineteen to twenty-six. They made such a favorable impression on me that I feel compelled to share the experiences in this chapter. I was struck by the consistent, positive behaviors they all exhibited, despite their diverse backgrounds and the various reasons they had for wanting to speak with me. Each of them demonstrated sincere *courtesy*, *curiosity*, and *gratitude*, and they all *followed up* with me in a timely manner based on the different subjects we had discussed. As an added bonus, each of them sent me a handwritten thank-you note. Why do these behaviors stand out? In today's world, I am likely to observe one, possibly two at most, of these behaviors I value so highly from people of *any* age, but rarely do I encounter all four behaviors at once. To say the least, I was intrigued and wanted to understand what made these four young adults different.

I reached out to each of them to specifically ask where they had learned these behaviors and who had taught them. Again, there was remarkable consistency from these four very different young adults as they answered my questions. Each of them described the positive influence of their parents growing up and later the influence of helpful mentors in college. The three who were out of college and in the workplace described a caring boss or senior-level mentor who had taken them under their wing and taught (and modeled) the value of courtesy, curiosity, gratitude, and follow-up. I suspected this would be the case, but it was affirming to hear it straight from these remarkable young people.

Mentorship is a virtue. Why? It involves the noble investment in actively using our knowledge and experience to support the growth and development of others, demonstrating qualities like generosity, compassion, and a commitment to helping others succeed. There are two roles in a mentor relationship: the mentor and the mentee.

The Role of the Mentor

I am truly grateful to have had the opportunity to frequently speak on college campuses and mentor early career professionals over the last two decades. I have heard for years the criticism leveled at this emerging generation of future leaders by older professionals who bemoan what they perceive to be a lack of interest in practicing the positive behaviors I share in this chapter. At times I have been critical as well. Maybe though, if the lessons from these four young adults means anything, we should point the finger of blame at ourselves and not them. *Maybe the students were ready all along and the teachers were nowhere to be found . . .*

Those of us who are parents have a wonderful opportunity to teach our children the lessons and values that will make them successful in life and in the professional world. Do we make the most of this opportunity and the short amount of time we have them under our roofs to achieve this goal? For those of us who are leaders, do we look at our younger colleagues with a jaundiced eye and level unfair criticism at them—or do we embrace our clear responsibility to teach them what we have learned and prepare them to lead? Do we actively give time to students in the schools we attended or in the communities where we live? How many early career colleagues at work are we mentoring right now? How much time do we invest in sharing lessons and stories from our career with junior members of our company, illuminating the keys to our success and helping them learn from our failures? By the way, I would suggest that we not wait for the perfect company program to act, but instead treat mentorship as the urgent and ongoing responsibility of every leader.

I hope that as you read this chapter, you will feel *encouraged* and *inspired* to be the positive mentor young adults and early career professionals will identify one day in the future as someone who helped, guided, taught, and coached them to success. I know my younger son has benefited tremendously from the generous mentors who have helped influence his life. With the demands of family, business, and other commitments, I sometimes fall short in this area, and you may be feeling the same. Regardless, most of us can do better. Surely we can find time to invest in the future. Even if we start with mentoring just one college student or early career professional after reading this chapter, that will be a start. Don't let uncertainty or self-doubt get in the way: I believe *everyone* has something of value to share with others.

If you are already an encouraging and helpful mentor to the next generation of leaders, then I would like to share my sincere gratitude. If you have gifts, wisdom, and lessons to share and are willing to find time to share them, please take on this challenge without delay. Finally, I have a surprise to share that good mentors already know: As we spend time mentoring early career colleagues, *they typically inspire and teach us valuable lessons as well.*

The Role of the Mentee

If you are an early career professional, I strongly encourage you to proactively seek out mentorship. The mentee's role is to take responsibility for their own learning and development and work with their mentor to achieve their goals. The early formative years of your career can be filled with rewarding learning experiences and amazing opportunities if you tap into the experience and wisdom of more senior leaders around you. Be respectful, be specific in your request for their time, be a great listener, and make the most of the opportunity to be mentored. Refer to Chapter 2 and the advice on accountability for insights on how to be accountable in these mentor relationships.

Embrace the virtue of mentorship at every stage of your career. In my experience, the mentees who made their most of their mentorship opportunity early in the career have become outstanding mentors to others as they grow in seniority. That is my sincere hope for you.

What valuable insights from your life and experiences can you share with an aspiring leader today? If you are an early career professional, what areas of your life and career would benefit from the sound advice of a helpful mentor? Identify who you think can help you and make a goal of approaching them and securing their help over the next thirty days.

CHAPTER 19

Morality

The Need for a Moral Compass

∽

We are in the middle of a profound sea of change affecting all aspects of life: social, cultural, economic, and political. Changes are being played out all over the world. Prompted by the alienation and uncertainty of our age, people—now more than ever—want to find a reliable moral compass. They want to integrate their whole selves; integrate who they are with what they do. Some are coming to recognize a deep-seated drive within each one of us to use our talents, intelligence and imagination for the greater good.

FROM A TALK GIVEN BY THE LATE JAMES L. NOLAN, AUTHOR OF
DOING THE RIGHT THING AT WORK

Nearly every company has a values statement, but rarely can the typical employee recite it—or even articulate the ways the company practices those values. Values should be more than a plaque on a wall or a bulleted list on a website. They are guiding principles and serve as our inner voice to advise us about what is right or wrong. It is important that personal and professional values are integrated and aligned.

A finely tuned moral compass can provide us with a set of core values that help guide our decisions throughout our lives. Ideally, there should be a balance between what is good for us and what is good for our company (and society in general).

Leaders are not likely to begin their careers with a fully developed moral compass. The virtue of morality and good ethical judgment is learned and cultivated over the course of a career. Over time, a person's moral compass will likely evolve based on some combination of faith, life experiences, relationships, and the simple passage of time. Leaders with a strong moral compass will work hard to live up to their values and make sure the colleagues and clients in their circle of influence will always feel the positive impact of those values. My moral compass has largely been determined by how I was raised by my parents, my life and work experiences, the crucible of adversity, helpful mentors, friends who challenge me, and my strong faith. How about you?

The most important aspect of having a moral compass is actually *using* that moral compass. If we invest in developing a moral compass and then ignore what it tells us or never read it at all, I hope we can agree it does us absolutely no good. By "reading" our moral compass, I simply mean thoughtfully and logically considering our choices in a given situation and making sure our internal values and ethics square up with the decisions we make. Are they well aligned or are they in conflict?

With leadership comes not only rights and privileges but also duties and obligations. I am making the basic assumption that if you're reading this book, you desire to accept these duties and obligations and to be men and women leaders of strong character who strive to do the right thing at work and serve the greater good, as my dear friend and mentor Jim Nolan described in the quote at the beginning of this chapter. Many of us are tired of the division, confusion, and anger so prevalent in society today and want to make a positive difference in the world (and in the workplace). If so, how do we continue to refine, develop, and use our moral compass? How do we apply these positive behaviors?

Six Ideas for Effectively Using Your Moral Compass

1. **Do you have the right list?** Clarify your core values. Write a list of what they are, then modify your behavior to work with your values rather than against them. Distinguish between your *aspirational* values and your *actual* values. In other words, there are values you truly live day in and day out and other values you aspire to achieve but have yet to act on. I recommend that your list of actual core values be five or less.

2. **Ask the right questions.** To find out if the core values you have selected are ones you actually live and act on, ask yourself the following questions: *Are you willing to* fight *for them? Are you willing to* sacrifice *for them? Are you willing to* spend time *on them? Are you willing to* share *them publicly with others?* By wrestling with and eventually answering these questions, you can begin the journey of discovering what really matters to you, aligning your actions with your core values, and raising your expectations for how business can be a positive force in our society.

3. **Navigate the challenges.** There will often be stress and negative pressure associated with situations and encounters where you need to rely on your moral compass and make the right decisions. It can feel like a shock to the system if you are not prepared. The capacity to manage these challenges will be critical to your long-term success in living out your values in the workplace.
4. **Resist excuses.** "Everybody else is doing it." "It's not my responsibility." "It's not that big of a deal, and we should let it go this time." "I am afraid of the ramifications if I speak up." When you ignore your moral compass and hide your values in the face of challenging ethical situations, you are making harmful compromises that eat away at you and diminish your overall leadership. Resist this temptation. Take a stand.
5. **Keep it simple.** The mere idea of engaging your moral compass may invoke perceptions of a standard that is almost impossible to achieve. Far from it! Consider focusing on the small acts of good, ethical, and moral behavior that can help you make good use of your moral compass and develop your values at the same time. *Treat others well. Honor your commitments. Don't lie or mislead. Give proper credit where it is deserved. Practice servant leadership inside your company and in your community. Own your mistakes. Be humble.* These behaviors are basic yet powerful, and all of us are capable of exhibiting them each day. These behaviors

can also serve as a supportive foundation to help you make the more difficult choices that will inevitably come your way throughout your career.

6. **Be consistent and courageous.** Like it or not, fully utilizing the moral compass you have carefully worked hard to build requires you to be a consistent role model. You can't ask others to follow an ethical and moral path in the workplace with certain expected behaviors if you are not willing to consistently do the same. That would be the worst form of hypocrisy. Be prepared at times to walk a lonely road. It takes courage to realize that you may sometimes be the only person willing to take a stand and do the right thing . . . and do it anyway.

I hope these six ideas will appropriately frame your thinking about ways to fully engage your moral compass. Utilizing your moral compass is important, but so is developing approaches to *strengthen* it. How do you strengthen your moral compass? Where can you go for help and encouragement?

Four Ideas for Strengthening Your Moral Compass

1. Seek out good mentors and role models. Who do you know who has a strong moral compass? Who models the right behaviors you wish to emulate? Who can you turn to for answers to your difficult ethical or moral questions? Reflect carefully about your current work colleagues or professionals outside of your company who may be willing to spend time with you in a mentoring capacity. This can also include family and

close friends. Embrace and follow the advice given in the previous chapter on mentorship.

2. **Choose friends who will challenge you to grow.** Iron sharpens iron and men sharpen men, as the old saying goes. Choose your friends well. Spend quality time with people who will challenge you to grow your moral compass. For example, I am part of a Catholic men's group that I helped co-found in 2007. We are all businesspeople seeking practical ways to integrate our faith with our work. These good men are a great source of personal and spiritual growth for me, and I am grateful for their friendship and willingness to always challenge me to be a better father, husband, and business leader.

3. **Choose your environment wisely.** Sometimes you just don't fit a team or organization. You may have a feeling in the pit of your stomach that says you should just walk away because their values directly conflict with yours. Listen to that inner voice. If interviewing for a job, ask probing questions of the interviewer to get a feeling for their moral compass and the values of their organization. We all have to make a living, but we should never have to compromise our values or who we are to do so.

4. **Find a strong pillar to lean on.** The greatest source for clearly understanding what doing the right thing at work and in life looks like comes from my Catholic faith. My greatest source of strength comes from my active prayer life. My moral compass would

be greatly diminished if it was not fed daily by my life as a Christian. This is my example, but I know countless other professional men and women of all ages and backgrounds who would share similar views about their Christian, Jewish, Buddhist, Muslim, or other faith experiences. I am not saying people without faith are missing a moral compass. No, not at all! As long as your source of inspiration provides you with an *unchanging standard*, you're starting in the right place. It's unlikely that any two moral compasses are exactly alike, but most share common traits that can help you distinguish right from wrong.

A well-formed moral compass can help us strike the right balance in our lives between emotion and reason, idealism and practicality, and our needs and those of others. Simply put, a moral compass can and should guide us toward what we *ought* to do in a given situation, not just what we *want* to do—or even what other people want us to do. The strength of our moral compass helps us define our character, which determines how people choose to interact with us and contributes to the overall quality of our relationships. A strong moral compass is an essential strength of the leader who desires to consistently do the right things at work and in life.

It is fair to say that consistently using your moral compass can be extremely difficult and challenging. If you have a strong moral compass, does that mean you will never make mistakes or suffer through an ethical or moral stumble? I'm afraid not. Instead, those of us with a well-defined set of core values will be able to learn from those failings and use them to make better and more appropriate decisions in the future. In fact, it's often the situations that present adversity and test us that help our moral compass to grow stronger. This has certainly been my experience.

It sometimes feels as if the world has become a challenging place for men and women of goodwill to thrive. Many of us want to make a positive difference in the world, but we don't know where to begin. *Why not consider the workplace as a place to make a difference?* Displaying courage in the face of our polarized society's obstacles may seem overwhelming, but perhaps we should focus our attention on developing our moral compass and manifesting small acts of bravery to promote ethical and moral principles that are meaningful at work, where we spend so much of our adult lives. These small acts, in turn, can absolutely have a positive ripple effect on the bigger world around us.

Much of what you are reading in this book emanates from the moral compass I have endeavored to refine and utilize over the course of my career. I am far from perfect, and I assure you I have stumbled and made mistakes, but I keep on trying—and I encourage you to keep trying too. I promise the positive impact you will make on the people around you will make the effort well worth it.

How are you doing at embracing the virtue of morality in your own life? What steps will you take this week to develop and strengthen your moral compass?

CHAPTER 20

Patience

Six Best Practices for Being More Patient with Others

The practice of patience toward one another, the overlooking of one another's defects, and the bearing of one another's burdens is the most elementary condition of all human and social activity in the family, in the professions, and in society.

FR. LAWRENCE G. LOVASIK

I often think about the virtue of *patience* and the years I have spent trying to cultivate this habit I so admire and appreciate in others. As I was working on this book, I again reflected on this topic and a relevant conversation I recently had with a past coaching client. This busy senior leader in a large Atlanta-based company described his frustration and impatience with a number of people on his team and in his peer group. I listened carefully, then shared some hard-fought experience about being more patient with others from my own career and observations of others who I think do this well.

Here is a summary of the advice I offered this leader.

Putting myself in the shoes of others and seeing the world through their eyes has always been an effective approach to cultivating patience in my life. When I feel impatient with others, I try and force myself to realize that there may be understandable reasons for whatever they are doing to trigger my impatience and there is likely no malicious intent. I work hard at not responding in the moment, especially if I am frustrated or impatient, and make a sincere effort to understand why they are saying or doing the thing that is evoking this response in me. I assure you that I am not always successful, but it gets easier as I get older.

This idea of better understanding others, walking in their shoes and seeing the world through their eyes is all becoming countercultural in today's world. I work with business professionals every day who are dealing with ever-increasing levels of stress and anxiety, overscheduled workdays, little time for meaningful conversations and nurturing relationships, and neglect for their own self-care. Lack of patience with others is a likely fruit of these environments and approaches to work/life. If this chapter is resonating and you want to improve your level of patience with others, here are **six best practices** to consider:

1. **Be Present.** When engaging with work colleagues, friends, family or whoever, put the smartphone away and completely focus on the person or people in front of you. Schedule adequate time for these conversations. When your thoughts are occupied by your next

appointment or to-do item, your impatience rises and you are only thinking about the future and not those deserving of your full attention. If at all possible, have conversations in-person; reading facial expressions and listening to the tone of each other's voice improves the quality of all dialogue. Virtual meetings, with the camera on, are an acceptable alternative if there is no other option.

2. **Be Curious.** You have to ask questions to truly understand why people think a certain way or do what they do. Ask how they are doing at work and outside of work. Ask them to explain their reasoning on decisions. Ask them if they understand your expectations. Ask them if they need help and how you can better support them. Curiosity activates greater understanding and reduces impatience.

3. **Actively Listen.** When we are struggling with patience, listening can be very difficult. If we are genuinely curious, it follows that we also need to be good listeners. We may be learning the all-important "whys" behind behaviors that are making us feel impatient with others. Be mindful to not listen only until it is your turn to speak, but listen to better understand.

4. **Practice a Little Self-Reflection.** Look in the mirror: Am I to blame for my lack of patience with others? Did I adequately train/develop my team member(s)? Have I created clear expectations on what I want? Have I communicated clearly? Have I offered help and support? Did I explain the rules? Am I modeling the

behavior I wish to see in others? Am I stressed, anxious or burned out and is this why I am feeling impatient? Did I practice sincere curiosity to perhaps learn of a personal burden my colleague or team member is carrying on their shoulders? Wasn't I once in the same situation as the person in front of me?

5. **Sleep on It.** When feeling impatient with others, if possible, it is always a good idea to not respond right away. Take a little time, perhaps twenty-four hours, to carefully consider all angles of the situation. Allow yourself to gain a sense of calm and peace. Word to the wise: Responding when impatient, frustrated or angry is *never* a good idea. Also, avoid responding when feeling impatient via email or text (see best practice #1). I have learned over the years the tremendous benefits of this best practice.

6. **"Do unto Others . . ."** The Golden Rule is an obvious and critical best practice for us to follow. We should be motivated to be more patient with others because we all need others to be patient with us. Reflect for a moment on how you personally benefited from someone being patient with you. How did you feel? Did you thank them? Let these positive experiences in your life inform and motivate your own practice of patience with the people you encounter each day.

I often write about the importance of being good humans. Practicing patience with others helps us become more understanding, compassionate, and empathetic, and it fosters stronger relationships. Patience is a powerful virtue. Patience is an act of kindness. Our patience is a wonderful gift we can give others.

The people I admire and respect most in my personal and professional life are all incredibly patient. I am always a work in progress and have a number of areas I wish to improve, but perhaps in the coming days I will simply focus on more intentionally practicing the virtue of patience. I hope this effort inspires others to do the same . . . and I pray they will also be more patient with me.

> *How would you assess your ability to be patient? Have you tried putting yourself in the shoes of others to better understand their behavior and motivations? Identify one person toward whom you are currently feeling impatience. Using the best practices in this chapter, work on showing them (and others who trigger you) more patience in the coming weeks.*

CHAPTER 21

Reflection

Don't Be Afraid to be Countercultural

༄

I'm very concerned that our society is much more concerned with information than wonder, in noise rather than silence. How do we encourage reflection? . . . Oh my, this is a noisy world.
MISTER ROGERS

I wrote much of what you are reading in this chapter several months ago after waking up early on a Saturday morning to gaze at a stunning sunrise in the Blue Ridge Mountains of Georgia from the back porch of a house my family rented for a weekend getaway. In the predawn light, the sun gradually rose from behind the mountains in front of me and cast its beautiful light on the scattered clouds in hues of orange and purple before it fully emerged with all its intense brilliance. The only noise I heard was the chatter of birds as I sipped my coffee and let my mind wander while I pondered this gift from our Creator. It was the perfect time and place to reflect on the book and life in general.

I have been on an intentional journey to more fully embrace

the practice of reflection for the last several years, but the path has often been difficult and filled with obstacles. We are easily caught up in the daily grind of work racing from meeting to meeting, and our lives outside of work are often equally as busy. We are surrounded by noise and distractions, and quiet moments are rare. We don't experience often enough the moments of peace and beauty like the one I described in the first paragraph. The smartphone, computer, and TV screens we gaze at all day long can become electronic pacifiers if we're not careful, and I fear we are at risk of morphing into tragic creatures resembling Gollum from *The Lord of the Rings* as he looks with obsessive longing at his "Precious." Think I am exaggerating? Try going twenty-four hours with no screen time of any kind and see how your brain reacts.

If you are willing to introduce more reflection time into your life and want to activate this virtue, I encourage you to carefully ponder all the various chapters in this book. You might want to go back and reread the ones that resonated most, and I encourage you to do the action/challenges I pose at the end of each chapter as they are all rooted in reflection. Here are **three additional ideas** to consider that will also help you to foster your practice of the virtue of reflection:

1. **Be intentional about creating boundaries during the workweek.** Don't let your workdays be a continuous series of back-to-back meetings and other task-related activities without creating small windows of protected time set aside for deeper thinking, exercise, reading, listening to music, time with friends and loved ones, or

anything else that gives you energy. Consider waking up a little earlier each day and using that quiet time for prayer or meditation. Schedule this time and protect it as you would your most important business meetings and don't allow nonessential busywork to creep in. This practice not only promotes reflection but also helps avoid burnout.

2. **Go device-free from time to time.** I know it is difficult in today's connected world, but turn off the screens every now and then. Put away the smartphone and shut down the computer more often, especially during nonwork hours. Call a colleague—or even better, meet them in-person—rather than send an email. Read a book instead of watching TV. Experience the outdoors, even if you only take a walk in your neighborhood. A great start is to establish small device-free zones each day, such as early morning, lunchtime and dinnertime, and then expand from there. It will feel uncomfortable at first, but I encourage you to commit to replacing a portion of your screen time with something healthy, natural, and real.

3. **Spend quality in-person time with others. Have a drink with an old friend or coffee with a business colleague.** Go to sporting events with them. Savor meals with family and friends. Join other volunteers and give your time to a worthy cause. Take long walks with your significant other. Go on fun trips. Real in-person conversations or even quiet moments with the significant people in your life offer a much-needed

respite from the noise and craziness of the world. This also helps you create memorable moments upon which to reflect.

Why Is This Important?

If you create space and time for this deeper thinking, it will absolutely help you lead a richer and fuller life. Practicing the virtue of reflection is not only good for your mental and physical health—it will help you become a better human being. You will be more keenly aware of your surroundings and the different people you encounter each day, and you will recognize more clearly the opportunities you have to make a positive difference in this world.

I know that in our fast-paced, technology-driven, and social media-saturated world, promoting the virtue of reflection is a little countercultural. Learning from the past . . . being more fully present in the moment . . . focusing on being good human beings. . . . These ideas may seem alien in today's world and out of sync with the culture, but that is exactly why I chose to include this chapter on reflection and share it with you. No matter where you are in your career and whatever generation you belong to, I believe you will benefit from the advice and lessons you have read—and hopefully increase your own practice of reflection.

How will you more intentionally create opportunities for reflection in your life? Begin by identifying obstacles in your life to reflection, then methodically remove or reduce them in the months ahead.

CHAPTER 22

Relationship Building

Essential Lessons for Building Better Business Relationships

☙

Living a connected life leads one to take a different view. Life is less a quest than a quilt. We find meaning, love, and prosperity through the process of stitching together our bold attempts to help others find their own way in their lives. The relationships we weave become an exquisite and endless pattern.
KEITH FERRAZZI, AUTHOR OF *NEVER EAT ALONE*

I have long been a keen student of the *essential tactics* and *simple engagement* approaches that are critical for building effective business relationships both inside and outside our organizations. Nothing gets better simply because we wish it, and this certainly applies to how we approach relationships in the business world. There are no magic answers and few shortcuts to being great at relationship building. Improvement takes hard work, self-discipline, intentionality, and commitment. It takes a willingness to change old habits and develop new approaches. Also, it takes the recognition that sometimes focusing on the basics and embracing simplicity often work best.

Essential Tactics

Here are **ten essential tactics** I have found to be the most consistently helpful in effectively activating the virtue of relationship-building over the course of my career:

1. **Embrace your personality style.** I have known for decades that I am a high-functioning introvert. Instead of following conventional wisdom and attending countless anxiety-producing networking events, I have long pursued a one-on-one approach to meeting new people as well as meeting my existing network over coffee or lunch where I am more comfortable. I also try to end my meetings by 4:30 p.m. each day and get back to my home office to write, catch up on administrative work, exercise, and savor the alone time I need each day before engaging with my family.
2. **Leverage LinkedIn.** I have a simple rule: Everyone I encounter in person or by phone receives an invitation (always with a personal note providing context) to join my LinkedIn network within twenty-four hours of contact. This self-discipline helps me continuously add to my network with business professionals I encounter. LinkedIn provides a well-organized and convenient way to keep track of your network and provides easy access to their background information. The LinkedIn app is especially helpful when you need quick access to background information on your phone about someone you are meeting.

RELATIONSHIP BUILDING

3. **Nurture the network.** Nurture existing relationships at the same time you are expanding new ones. Much like a garden, healthy relationships must be maintained, and this takes work. The worst thing we can do is reach out to someone in our hour of need and realize that we failed to maintain the relationship. I keep a spreadsheet with every client, prospect, and business friend alphabetically listed with contact information and a section for notes. This helps me keep track of my large network, stay on top of required follow-up, and schedule future meetings.
4. **Put everything on the calendar.** Everything important in your life is likely scheduled, right? Why not treat your approach to business relationships the same way? My meetings, reminders about the topics of upcoming discussions, follow-up items, birthdays, anniversaries, etc., are all part of my calendar.
5. **Rethink how you spend your time.** If you see little time for building business relationships on your busy calendar, let me challenge you a bit. There are five opportunities a week for coffee or breakfast, five opportunities a week for lunch, and five opportunities for dinner. Start utilizing at least three or four of these fifteen opportunities each week to meet with someone new (or nurture an existing business relationship). You have to eat, so why not spend this time with another professional and accomplish two objectives during this time?
6. **Make it easy for them (not you).** If you are in "exploring" mode with a new business contact, if you

make the meeting time and venue as convenient as humanly possible for them, they are more likely to attend. This may mean before work, at lunch, or after work. In my experience, early coffee near their office is almost always the most convenient time and place. Your convenience is *not* as important as theirs in the early phases of relationship building.

7. **Embrace the basics.** Always be courteous. Always be grateful. Acknowledge that you know the other person is investing valuable time in meeting you and you appreciate this. The basics always work, and this is as basic as it gets! Follow up in a timely manner with a thank-you note (an email is okay, but not as memorable).

8. **Focus on relationships, not acquaintances.** Meeting someone only once at best makes them an acquaintance, *not* a relationship. This is one of the reasons I cringe at the thought of collecting fifty business cards at networking events. You have to invest energy and thought into having multiple meetings with someone that you both see as beneficial.

9. **Be personal.** Meeting someone for the first time? Not sure what to say? Do you desire a meaningful conversation about real issues and not the usual surface or politically correct dialogue? Be transparent first. Get personal (with discernment). Be authentic. If you desire someone to open up to you, you should be open about your life first. In effect, if you take the first step in sharing, this gives the other person "permission" to be open about topics outside of work.

10. **Always make deposits.** I encourage my clients to view their business networks as a "relationship economy." In this economy, you should be consistently offering to help and investing (making deposits) in the people in your business network. A day will come when you may be in need of help, a favor, or maybe just a listening ear, and you will have an easier time making a "withdrawal" if you have been making deposits along the way.

A Simple Three-Step Approach to Engagement

Before my father retired, he was a master of the virtue of relationship building and was well-respected and trusted by all who knew him throughout his long career. I remember well the advice he gave me many years ago when I graduated from the University of Georgia and was about to begin my own business career. He told me to think about three basic approaches when I was encountering new professionals as I began my first post-college job:

1. Be helpful; serve their needs.
2. Be sincerely curious.
3. Always add value.

It took me a few years to fully grasp the importance of what he told me, but his sage advice is at the core of how I have approached my relationships over the course of my career. Here is what my father's simple wisdom has come to mean to me today.

Be helpful; serve their needs. My father's first tip was to approach everyone with a *servant's heart*. My parents were servant leaders throughout their lives, so I was fortunate to have this behavior modeled for me from a very young age. When you make your efforts about sincerely helping others and serving their needs, you will find relationship building to be a worthwhile, fulfilling experience that will ultimately come back to you in positive and unexpected ways. When it is all about you and your needs, people see through that, and your attempts at relationship building can become a miserable, laborious experience on many levels. Sincerely ask, "Is there anything I can do to help you?" or simply do something for them out of generosity with no expectation of return. As my father used to say, "Always make it about them, not about you."

Be sincerely curious. My father's second tip stemmed from his understanding that meeting a lot of senior businesspeople might make me feel intimidated and nervous. He encouraged me to be genuinely curious about others as a helpful way to counter my lack of experience and my misguided view that I needed to have all the answers. I have learned that people find us more interesting when we ask them questions. They appreciate the humility when someone genuinely wishes to learn something new or just desires to know them better. If you're stuck on knowing the perfect thing to say, *ask questions*. If you want to impress a client, new friend, or colleague and learn important information about them, *ask questions*. Being curious takes the pressure off and stimulates a more engaging and balanced conversation. We would all be well served to embrace humility and do less telling and more asking.

Always add value. My dad's final tip was a little difficult for me to understand when I was twenty-one, and it took me a few years to finally get it. He encouraged me to always approach every meeting with the mindset that I owned the responsibility for the other person to feel the meeting was well worth their time. He encouraged me to find ways to add value to every conversation or meeting. Today, this concept of adding value takes many forms: being a good listener, offering helpful advice, making a connection to someone in my network, giving the gift of a book, or following up with a helpful article related to our conversation. This particular tip, when practiced well, almost always generates numerous follow-up meetings that lead to strong relationships and even close friendships.

This simple approach to engagement and the "essential tactics" I shared earlier have proven to be invaluable in my desire to build authentic business relationships. These concepts work well with internal company relationships as well as with those outside your organization. Don't over complicate or add unnecessary layers to relationship building. Develop a simple and actionable approach that works for you. Just be yourself, be helpful, be curious, and add value while utilizing the tactics I have shared. I promise this ongoing investment in mastering the virtue of relationship building will be one of the most rewarding and satisfying efforts of your career.

Pick one of the essential tactics and make it your focus this week. Evaluate the impact this has on your relationships and then pick another to focus on the following week. Keep doing this until you have tried and mastered them all.

CHAPTER 23

Self-Discipline

The Power of Self-Discipline and Intentionality
for Busy Professionals

*The key is not to prioritize your schedule,
but to schedule your priorities.*
STEPHEN R. COVEY

If you and I were to have a calm conversation about priorities away from the hustle and bustle of the daily work environment, we would likely list the usual suspects. For me, my top priorities (in this order) are faith, family, health, and work. You may have a similar list that accurately captures what matters most to you. These *aspirational* priorities sound good, feel good, and we genuinely wish to honor them, but they often enter into brutal conflict each week with the challenging demands of our jobs. We often wind up giving the important priorities outside of work the scraps of time left over from our busy workdays. On the aspirational priority list, work may be last. On the actual priority list, work is often the top priority.

I would suggest that the practical way to address this critical issue is considering how to practice the virtue of self-discipline and embrace intentionality. We likely know what we need and want to do, but we may struggle to get it all done. Perhaps one of the best places to start is considering where we spend our time and then develop useful routines. Let me give you an example.

For many years, I have been intentional about preparing at the beginning of each day to be at the top of my game for clients, friends, and family. I have been an early riser since childhood, and my early morning ritual has been consistent for the last few decades. While some people like to exercise early in the day, I prefer to work out at lunch or late in the afternoon as a form of stress release and use my early morning time for prayer, deep thinking, reading, and creative writing. I wake up at 4:45 a.m. every day and enjoy the first of my two cups of coffee. I say a prayer and do some spiritual or business reading, always looking to feed and expand my mind. I have a healthy breakfast, enjoy a second cup of coffee, and do some writing, usually a blog post or a chapter for a future book. I sometimes work on creating new leadership development content for my business. Around 6:15 a.m., I check on the news of the day, send a few emails, manage administrative aspects of my business, and prepare for my first meeting, which is typically at 7:00 or 7:30 a.m. Monday through Friday. I follow a similar routine on the weekends—without the early meetings and emails, of course.

This focused routine prepares me to fully engage with the leaders I work with and be an alert and active listener/coach attuned to their needs. I feel sharp, creative, and focused, and I credit this intentional and disciplined approach to starting the day for allowing me to give the best of myself to others. I am grateful that my business has thrived over the years, in part because of this morning ritual and its impact on my day. Note: I followed this same routine pre-COVID-19, but I typically left my home by 6:45 or 7:00 a.m. each weekday to drive to my first coffee meeting of the day.

Two of the keys to improving self-discipline, mastering intentionality, and developing routines is practicing *self-awareness* and learning how to *say no*. For example, I have known most of my life that I am naturally sharpest and have the most energy in the morning. As a high-functioning introvert, I also know I will be at my best engaging with others from 7:00 a.m. to around 4:00 p.m. most days. I am typically scheduled with individual clients or leadership teams the vast majority of each day Monday through Friday. Because high-functioning introverts tend to run out of energy for people by mid to late afternoon, I carve out thirty to forty minutes for exercise (usually intense cardio) between 11:00 a.m. and 1:00 p.m. every day, and I also take a two-mile walk at the end of the workday (weather permitting) before dinner with my family. These exercise windows allow me to relieve stress, partially restore my energy for people, and contribute significantly to my overall mental health and physical fitness. The end-of-the-day walk is particularly important to me as I turn my phone off, engage in prayer, and use the remaining walking time for deep thinking and reflection. I have also recently added a thirty-minute window for reading after my, walk which has been very helpful. I am then ready to fully engage with my family at dinner and be present for them the rest of the evening.

I am self-aware about my needs, but I have also worked hard for years at learning to effectively and respectfully say no. The exercise time on my calendar is the time slot I work hardest to protect. It has been a fixture on my calendar since early 2020, and I schedule all of my work around it. There are a few exceptions when I will move the exercise time, but they are rare. When I say no to someone who wants this protected time slot, I offer alternative times and do my best to be helpful and accommodate their request when it will work for both our calendars.

Why Does This Matter?

The leaders I admire and try to emulate are intentional about taking care of their physical, emotional, spiritual, and mental needs. They practice self-care wisely and excel at practicing the virtue of self-discipline. They understand (and I completely agree) that *you cannot share with others from an empty cup.*

One last tip to promote better self-discipline, intentionality, and useful routines is to place every important personal and professional goal or to-do on the calendar each week. This may seem obvious, but in my experience most businesspeople only schedule work-related items and fail to schedule the equally or more important personal stuff. The result is that the priorities and important areas of our personal lives only get the scraps of time left over from our hectic workdays. My advice is to *be more intentional.* Schedule everything important in your life (kid's activities, exercise, doctor visits, thinking time, prayer time, volunteering, anniversaries, birthdays, etc.) to ensure that nothing falls through the cracks. In my life, if something is on my calendar, it is highly likely to get done.

I don't pretend to have all the answers, and I often struggle to do all of this well like most businesspeople I know, but I keep trying to improve. Time is a precious resource, and we need to be good stewards of how we spend it. I believe greater intentionality, good routines, and embracing the virtue of self-discipline are the keys to igniting more success in life and business. If we achieve progress in making this a reality, life and work will be richer and more enjoyable because of our efforts.

How will you think differently about work and life this week and beyond? What steps can you begin making to develop better self-discipline, be intentional, and adopt healthy routines? How can you reinforce what is already working for you? Helpful tip: Find an accountability partner so you can challenge each other to make improvements, then frequently share your progress with them.

CHAPTER 24

Service

The Regular Heroes among Us

Some believe it is only great power that can hold evil in check, but that is not what I have found. It is the small everyday deeds of ordinary folk that keep the darkness at bay. Small acts of kindness and love. Why Bilbo Baggins? Perhaps because I am afraid, and he gives me courage.

GANDALF, *THE HOBBIT*

A blog post I received from a friend a few months before the publication of my 2022 book, *Upon Reflection*, contained a reference to the "ministry of obscurity." I found this to be quite profound if we apply that label to the millions of people around the world laboring every day to do good in their communities, being kind to others, raising their families, loving their neighbors, sharing their faith with others, caring for the sick, poor, and neglected, protecting us from harm, and leading virtuous lives—all in relative obscurity and seeking no recognition for their noble efforts. They are beacons of light who authentically practice the virtue of service in an increasingly angry and polarized world. Thinking about them gives me hope.

Through the countless conversations I have with others in my community and professional network, it is obvious that many of us feel let down and frustrated by politicians and public figures who espouse the right things but whose actions don't align with their words. Perhaps we are looking in the wrong places. Maybe for too long we have placed the wrong people on pedestals. It is entirely possible that we need look no further than our own families, workplaces, and communities for regular heroes to inspire us with their good examples.

They are all around us, but we may fail to notice them as it is easy to overlook the hardworking, virtuous, and generous among us. We may not always observe their good work and passion for serving others because they often go about doing the right things in quiet ways, avoiding the spotlight whenever possible. They care more about doing good than getting the credit. When they aren't working, they likely are spending quality time with their loved ones, serving others in the community, or investing in those they mentor. They provide a powerful witness in the simplest of actions.

In the weeks after I began pondering the idea of the ministry of obscurity, I encountered three people who I had the good fortune to see—*maybe for the first time*—as regular heroes quietly serving in this ministry. I have known who they are for years, but I was struck recently by how they are such good role models for me and others who know them.

Tom, a successful senior executive devoted to his church and his family, selflessly gives his time to a local homeless shelter

SERVICE

each month and organizes his church community to support it. He is a quiet and humble man who can always be counted on when someone needs help . . . and he coaches his daughter's soccer team for good measure.

Allison, a talented mid-level manager with a well-known consulting company, quietly devotes as much time as possible to helping job seekers and mentoring other early career professionals. She juggles all of this as a newlywed with the demands of a hectic job and has recruited her husband to help.

Finally, there is Sandy, the grandmother of a young man on the autism spectrum. Sandy started a nonprofit to help amazing young people like her grandson learn to communicate more effectively through improv and theater classes adapted to their style of learning. Her nonprofit has helped hundreds of people on the autism spectrum, and she is an inspiration to all who know her. She saw a need that was not being addressed in the autism community and took it upon herself to tackle it.

Regular heroes such as these three individuals and others like them are humble, selfless, and focused on how they can serve others. They are not necessarily trying to change the world, but instead they focus on helping and serving one person at a time. Here are five ways we can recognize these regular heroes:

1. They are **joyful** and **peaceful**, which naturally draws others to them.
2. They live **authentic** and **courageous** lives that do not change in the face of life's challenges.
3. They have a **generous spirit**; when engaging with others, it is always about you and not about them.

4. The folks I know who fit this category see the virtue of service they offer to others as a **duty** and **privilege** they are happy to carry out.
5. Their good work transcends politics and cultural whims. **Doing the right thing** for anyone in need is all that matters.

These regular heroes don't care who gets the credit. They pursue "eulogy virtue" versus "resume virtue," as described by author David Brooks in his book *The Road to Character*. Both types of virtues are important and worth pursuing and refining, but only eulogy virtues have any lasting value and legacy. For these selfless individuals, it's not about the glory or the fame. It's just a wonderful way to live.

I shared three examples of regular heroes laboring in the "ministry of obscurity" who grabbed my attention when I stopped seeking inspiration from those in the public arena and began looking at my own backyard and the people I encounter in my daily life. There are many other examples I could have also cited, such as the single mom working two jobs to support her young family, the foster parents who routinely take in and help troubled teens, and the teenager who organizes his friends to pick up trash on weekends to protect the environment and beautify his community. Who are the regular heroes living out the virtue of service in your world? What valuable lessons can you learn from them? Seek them out, share your sincere gratitude, and hopefully follow their great example.

Thank you to all who make the world a better place in your own quiet ways.

SERVICE

Consider the "regular heroes" in your life. What can you learn from them? How can you emulate their example? Keep a log of how many good acts you intentionally perform for two weeks where you receive no recognition other than directly from the recipients of your deeds. Reflect on how you feel after doing this and the positive impact you may have made on others. Make a commitment to increase your efforts and fully embrace the virtue of service in your life.

CHAPTER 25

Simplicity

Embracing Simplicity

There is no greatness where there is not simplicity, goodness, and truth.
LEO TOLSTOY, *WAR AND PEACE*

Do you ever feel overwhelmed with all the stress, responsibilities, and challenges in your daily life? If I am honest with myself, the times I feel most anxious or stressed are usually caused by my lifelong tendency to overcomplicate things and an inclination toward "busyness." As I grow older, I recognize the wisdom of something my parents often shared with me in my younger days: "Simplify your life."

Everything about our modern culture involves complexity and unnecessary layers. I long for more opportunities to live in the moment and experience life in "real time" versus the frantic pace I often keep. I want my legacy to be more than "He accomplished more than most"! I don't pretend to have all the answers, but I would like to share my three-step approach to achieve greater simplicity, peace, and a heightened sense of purpose in my life:

1. Have clear priorities.
2. Practice detachment.
3. Serve others.

Step One: Have Clear Priorities

"What are your priorities?" When I ask this question of other professionals, the answers are typically all over the map. I came into my Christian faith later in life. I went from a compartmentalized approach to living, unsuccessfully attempting to balance work and family, to a life where my faith is first, family is second, my health is third, and work is fourth on my list of priorities. Additionally, I work hard at keeping Christ at the center of everything I do, and the result is a more authentic and integrated approach to life where I am the same person at all times.

How Does This Play Out in My Life?

Faith—Through my active prayer life and worship, I do my best to serve the Lord and make sure He is my top priority. "Lord, help me to simplify my life by learning what you want me to be and becoming that person" (St. Thérèse of Lisieux).

Family—My vocation is to be the best husband and father possible. I serve my family by giving them my time, attention, and love. In our home, family dinner is a priority, as is the commitment my wife and I share in loving our children enough to challenge them with the truth. We have always worked hard to ensure that our children grow up with faith and strong values, and we consider it our duty to serve as role models for them.

Health—I cannot take my health for granted and must make exercise, diet, and rest a priority. I also have a responsibility to take care of my health so I can be present in the lives of my family for many years to come.

Work—I focus on sanctifying my work and pursuing excellence. I must remember that my vocation is not my career. My career exists to serve my family, not the other way around. My career provides a living for my family and is a way to fulfill my mission, but I cannot allow it to consume me in an unhealthy way.

Having our priorities straight requires intentionality and commitment . . . and a fair amount of courage. We must plan our time, decide on lines we won't cross, and stick to our principles. Most importantly, those of us who are Christians know we are made for heaven, not this world. We will be judged one day by *how* we lived, not how fast we lived. As C. S. Lewis said, "If I find in myself a desire which no experience in this world can satisfy, the most probable explanation is that I was made for another world."

Step Two: Practice Detachment

How do we detach? Does this mean we need to become hermits in a mountainside cabin? Of course not. But we need to acknowledge that we live in a materialistic and consumer-driven world that encourages us to acquire as much stuff as possible, often at the expense of what is truly important. If we can practice real freedom from the blind pursuit of an illusory better life attached to acquiring more material goods we don't need, we will be better prepared to make healthier and more meaningful choices in life. Also, remember that *attaching* ourselves to the right people and activities will further help us *detach* from the negative influences of this world.

Ideas for Pursuing Detachment:

- Let it go. Ask yourself if you really need "it," whatever "it" is. Will the bigger house, bigger car, and other toys truly make you happier? Or are you trying to fill an empty void in yourself with the wrong things?
- Be careful to not let your possessions/hobbies/interests become obstacles between you and your family or you and God.
- Be cognizant of what *enough* really means.
- Resist the siren call of the culture to become someone you are not.
- Recognize the virtue of hard work and reject the easy and responsibility-free life often promised by the world.
- Avoid the "pack mentality" and do what you know is right and true, not what everyone else is doing.
- Value true friends—the ones who challenge you, make you better, and don't require you to compromise who you really are. Be willing to accept having fewer friends in order to enhance your overall relationship health.
- Turn off the noise. Spend less time on your iPhone, TV, internet, podcasts, and talk radio and more time in quiet reflection, prayer, quality time with loved ones, physical exercise, and reading books.

- Frequently express gratitude for your blessings and all you have and never take your good fortune for granted.

I am challenged on a daily basis by the concept of detachment. It is very difficult to practice, yet when I do make progress in this area, I feel a profound sense of freedom and peace that encourages me to work harder at it every day. The world is constantly trying to pull me in the wrong direction. When I practice detachment from our culture and its more negative influences, I more clearly recognize and value the blessings I have received.

Step Three: Serve Others

What makes you tick? What are you called to do? Knowing who you are and what you are called to do is a critical component of simplifying your life. When I was in my twenties and thirties, I was focused on climbing the corporate ladder as fast as possible with little understanding of what I would do when I reached the top. As I shared in my third book, *Something More: The Professionals Pursuit of a Meaningful Life*, I walked away from a senior executive role with a billion-dollar restaurant company in my early thirties to run a boutique national executive search firm, and in 2013 I launched Serviam Partners, which offers executive coaching and leadership consulting services to companies and senior leaders. These career moves were all intentional and part of my ever-increasing desire to simplify my life and fully tap into my skills and passions in the service of others.

Probably the greatest revelation for me over the years has been the sense of peace and joy I feel that only comes from helping and serving other people. Even though I always seek to know, understand, and do God's will in my life, the times I most frequently feel close to achieving this are the times I do something in the service of others.

How Do I Serve Other People?

- As busy as I may be, I strive to make quality time for others.
- Treating others as I wish to be treated is a priority.
- try to be a good listener.
- I pray for others.
- I engage in civil discussions with those who disagree with me.
- Being candid is a gift when delivered with professionalism and love. I always try and give this gift to those I encounter.
- I connect others to helpful people and resources in my network.
- I try to give not only of my time but also of my talent and treasure to serve and help those less fortunate than me.
- I always try to add value to my relationships.
- I serve great causes and practice active stewardship with the help of my family and friends.

My giving to others is ultimately a gift right back to me. When I devote myself to helping a person in need, I feel a tremendous sense of fulfillment. My hectic schedule can sometimes get in the way, and I struggle to do all that I desire for others, but I keep trying.

Intentionality and Clarity Lead to Simplicity

When look back on your career, are you able to retrace your steps and reflect on lessons learned? At the beginning of my career, I was a follower, then I became a manager, and then a leader. Now I'm embracing the "influencer" stage of my career. Through my books, talks, coaching, and consulting, I strive to influence positive outcomes for the people I encounter in my life. I make mistakes, but I am clear about my goals and my desire to follow a simpler path, serve others, and live a faith-filled life. The path to get here had many twists and turns, but I've been very intentional along the way.

I hope you will reflect on the direction of your life and recognize that the time for embracing a simpler approach to life is *now*—not when you reach retirement. My encouragement to you is, simply put, to embrace the virtue of simplicity. You, your work, and everyone around you will benefit from this life-changing decision. While it is often a difficult struggle and countercultural, get rid of the excess and retain the necessary. Focus on what is important and have the right priorities. Serve others. Simplify.

How might you begin to live your life differently? What is one significant thing you can do to simplify your life in the days ahead?

CHAPTER 26

Stewardship

The Abundance Mindset Activates Stewardship

◈

The more principle-centered we become, the more we develop an abundance mentality, the more we are genuinely happy for the successes, well-being, achievements, recognition, and good fortune of other people. We believe their success adds to . . . rather than detracts from . . . our lives.
STEPHEN R. COVEY, *PRINCIPLE-CENTERED LEADERSHIP*

One of the many things I loved and admired about my mother was her generous nature and desire to help everyone she met. She worked very hard in her full-time job as well as in her more important roles as wife, mother, sister, daughter, and church volunteer—all while enduring numerous health-related issues in her later years. My mother dealt with all the stress, illness, and adversity in her life with joy and a smile . . . and never complained. In fact, she was always grateful and saw her challenges as blessings, not burdens. She always had a kind word for others or some sort of encouragement to offer in spite of what might be described as overwhelming burdens to carry. She was always a great steward of her gifts and never hesitated to share them. The virtue of being a good steward of our time, talent, and treasure is certainly not new, but my mother's joyful and exemplary practice of this virtue was activated and nurtured by her *abundance mindset*.

Abundance versus Scarcity

I encounter people every day in my professional and personal life who exhibit either an abundance mindset or a scarcity mentality, which is the opposite of abundance and makes good stewardship very difficult. Leadership guru Stephen R. Covey initially coined these terms in his bestselling book, The *7 Habits of Highly Effective People*. Scarcity mentality is about seeing life as a pie, meaning that if one person takes a big piece of the pie, it leaves less for everyone else to enjoy. It seems that in the business world, many of us who are fortunate to be leaders have been conditioned to have a scarcity mentality. When we feel overwhelmed by the demands of our calendar, the challenges of finding good talent, an unexpected pandemic, or the normal stress of life, we may find ourselves in self-protective mode, being stingy with our time and hoarding our resources. We may be reluctant or unable to see our opportunity and obligation as leaders to look beyond our own problems, show kindness and encouragement, generously share of ourselves with others, and motivate or inspire. A scarcity mentality may be keeping many of us from achieving our goals and the success we crave, but more importantly from experiencing the richer, fuller, and more noble life the abundance mindset can offer.

Two Examples

Several months ago, I had the opportunity to experience clear examples of the abundance and scarcity approaches in the same day. My oldest son, Alex, has been employed as a part-time employee for over eight years by a global retail company at one of their stores near our home. Alex came down with the flu and had to miss work for the first time in his working life. I called the store to let them know Alex would be out of work while he recovered. The assistant store manager was very kind during our brief call and conveyed his hope for a speedy recovery. Within five minutes of that call, the store manager called, and my wife answered the phone. He spent twenty minutes with her, asking about Alex, informing her that Alex would be paid for the hours he missed, and sharing how much he and the entire team valued him. He also shared a few specific stories about Alex's hard work and how much respect he had for my son. What makes this story remarkable—and a good illustration of abundance—is that this gentleman was under enormous stress. His store, one of the busiest in the company, was understaffed, impacted by supply chain issues, and the recent flu outbreak had significantly impacted his remaining team. Despite all of this, his first thought was to call the family of a part-time employee and show kindness, encouragement, and gratitude. He operated from a place of abundance when he easily could have wallowed in his scarcity.

Later that same day, I had a call with a business leader who was interested in me working with her and her team. I learned on our call that the team had experienced high turnover and was dealing with a host of challenges that were exacerbated by a challenging economic climate. I also heard from this leader how busy she was (with seemingly no control over her calendar), the long hours she worked, the stress she was feeling at home, and how much she disliked her boss. It was also her perception that the team complained a lot and wanted more time from her than she could afford to give. I took all this in and asked for her permission to share an observation. I respectfully challenged her that she was operating out of a scarcity mindset that was negatively impacting her team and her personal performance. We walked through possible steps she could take to reclaim her calendar and build air into her schedule, which would help her to invest in the team and elevate her leadership to the abundance mindset. To her credit, she realized during our conversation that she had become somewhat blinded by her own significant challenges and had lost sight of her obligations as a leader to invest in her team. I share this example with her permission, and we kicked off a coaching engagement a few weeks later.

Always Show Up with a Gift . . . and Other Helpful Ideas

As you think about your desire to be a good steward of your gifts and lead with an abundance mindset more consistently, I would like to share four helpful ideas to reinforce abundance thinking:

1. **Always show up with a gift.** From the time I was a little boy, I remember my mother's frequent advice to "always bring a gift and never show up empty-handed" when meeting with someone. I used to think she meant only tangible gifts like flowers, a book, or a plate of brownies. As I grew older and watched her in action, I began to realize that her brilliant advice meant so much more and included sharing gifts of kindness, encouragement, candor, connections, mercy, forgiveness, gratitude, good counsel, and inspiration with everyone we meet in our business or personal lives. Now I try to never show up empty-handed and always be willing to share my gifts.
2. **Be grateful.** Always live and lead with gratitude. When we operate with a grateful mindset, we better appreciate what we have and are more inclined to share with others. This attitude of gratitude should also extend to appreciating our burdens and challenges, not just our blessings and good fortune.
3. **Practice agape love.** *Agape* is "unconditional love." It is expressed by individuals who offer respect, understanding, and compassion to all beings without hesitation, judgment, or conditions. Practicing this type of love without expectations or self-benefit is a wonderful way to practice abundance and is a key aspect of good stewardship.
4. **Recognize that leadership has responsibilities and obligations.** To be a leader is not just about having followers. To be a leader places special obligations and

responsibilities on those of us fortunate to carry this title. It means we are required to serve and help others in our charge, but also to operate through this lens in all areas of our lives. Truly effective leaders who embrace this definition of leadership operate out of abundance, not scarcity, and a ripple effect of positivity and goodness that emanates from their efforts.

As I mentioned in the opening paragraph, a powerful lesson my mother taught me during her long life—and one I observe in other successful leaders who practice abundance—is to live life as a steward, not an owner. This is a simple yet profound belief. To act with more abundance and be generous, we should acknowledge that we are not really the owners of anything we have been entrusted with in this world. If we faithfully practice the virtue of stewardship and embrace an abundance mindset, we will find ample opportunities every single day to share these gifts even when life seems hard, and we can't see beyond our own challenges.

A good steward with an abundance mindset feels more positive, empowered, confident, and focused on serving others. They have opened themselves up to giving generously of themselves and their gifts. Someone with a scarcity mindset may feel overwhelmed, anxious, and frustrated with their life. They may find it difficult to share, give, or invest in others. We all have an option today to embrace abundance or scarcity as we interact with and lead those around us. Which will it be? And remember . . . always show up with a gift!

STEWARDSHIP

Reflect on the last thirty days. Have you been a good steward of your time, talent, and treasure? When have you exhibited either the abundance or scarcity mindset? How might you have shown up in a different way? Think about how you will utilize the tips in this chapter to embrace an abundance mindset more intentionally going forward.

CHAPTER 27

Thankfulness

Making the Most of a Once-Treasured Practice

Making the extra effort to say thanks in a genuine, personal manner goes a long way. It is pleasurable to do, and it encourages more of the same good behaviors.
RICHARD BRANSON

I was having coffee with three friends not long ago, and we had an interesting discussion about the topic of gratitude . . . specifically, thank-you notes. I shared with them that I had recently received a wonderful handwritten thank-you note from a mentee of mine. I shared how I knew this early career professional, what development areas we were working on, and what specifically had prompted the note. When I finished, I asked each of them to share a little about the last handwritten thank-you note they had received and exactly how they felt when they received it.

What struck me as interesting was the warm smile each

of them had as they described the note and who it was from, why they had received it, and the positive way the note made them feel. I then asked them to describe the last thank-you message they had received via email or text. The difference in their responses was markedly different. They were truly appreciative of the thank-you messages, but their descriptions were more perfunctory, and these messages were deleted along with the other read emails or text messages they received that day. It is also interesting to note that each of them keeps the handwritten thank-you notes they receive. I practice the same habit and have a box full of them in my home office.

Why is this important?

I have long shared with clients, friends, college students, and early career professionals the importance of the handwritten thank-you note and the practice of the virtue of thankfulness. I know it sounds old-fashioned, but this is one of the best ways to make a favorable impression on another person. Emailed and texted thank-you messages are nice, but they are soon deleted and forgotten. Handwritten notes are memorable. Thank-you notes are special, and I read them (and reread them), and it makes me think warmly about the other person—which is really the whole point.

If you want to be viewed more positively than your colleagues at work as you look to advance in your career or fare better than others interviewing for jobs you are interested in, consider the power and impact of the simple handwritten thank-you note. I can share from experience and observation that the extra effort and thoughtfulness associated with this once-common tradition will make you stand out favorably in the eyes of the recipient. Wouldn't you like to have been one of the individuals positively discussed in the coffee meeting I mentioned with my friends, all of whom are senior business leaders?

Not everything is worthy of a handwritten thank-you note, and in fact, the majority of the time emailed and texted thank you messages are more than sufficient (especially for employees of global companies). I certainly send my share of gratitude via email and text each week. We should also be consistently expressing our sincere thanks verbally and in the moment . . . which is hopefully a given. But every now and then, an impactful encounter, helpful conversation, or kind act will merit the investment of time in a heartfelt and thoughtful written note of gratitude sent in a timely manner.

What actually merits a handwritten thank-you note? In my opinion, here are some relevant examples:

- After every first interview and if you accept a job offer. All interviewers and your new boss should receive a handwritten note of thanks from you.
- When a busy senior leader makes time to meet with you to further your development.
- If you receive a promotion or unexpected pay raise.
- When you receive wise and impactful counsel from a work colleague or friend.
- ALWAYS after receipt of an unexpected gift—and all gifts received on your special days.
- In response to any acts of kindness where someone

has gone out of their way to do something special and helpful for you.
- When someone commits a truly selfless act, shows courage, or demonstrates sincere care and concern for others, send a thank-you note to acknowledge their goodness . . . even if it didn't directly impact you.
- If you hear a great speaker or read something by an author that really impacts you, send them a note if you can find their address.
- Send handwritten thank-you notes to customers and clients to share your appreciation for their business and partnership.
- Write thank-you notes to your employees and colleagues a few times a year, especially at Thanksgiving, to express how much you appreciate them; thank them for some specific aspect of their performance when appropriate.

Here are **seven helpful tips** to elevate your practice of sending handwritten thank-you notes:

1. Invest in quality stationary, personalized if possible
2. Be specific. Avoid vagueness and share exactly what prompted your note and why you are grateful.
3. **Be careful with spelling, grammar, and penmanship.** I know this is obvious, but be very careful with spelling, grammar, and neatness; ask someone you trust to proof your note if possible. A handwritten note that misses the mark in these areas can work against you

and leave a poor impression. If you are concerned about your penmanship, you might try typing a short letter to include in your thank-you card and just sign the bottom of the note. Handwritten is always best, but I have seen this alternative, and it is a suitable replacement if necessary.

4. **Be a good detective and track down their address.** Corporate addresses are easily available online. If the individual works from home (this is obviously more common these days), politely ask them for their address and let them know you plan to follow up. If this feels a little uncomfortable, reach out to their administrative assistant if they have one and ask for the address. Also, if you *really* want to make a positive impression on a senior leader, drop the handwritten note off in person at their office the next day with their assistant (if this is geographically possible).

5. **Have a goal of writing at least four handwritten thank-you notes per month.** If we are paying attention and acting with intention, we should be able to find appropriate reasons to send at least four notes a month.

6. **Remember that this is a best practice regardless of your generation, experience level, or title.**

7. **Take a moment and consider how you are making the other person feel with your note.** This perspective goes beyond how it affects you. You are showing them gratitude and appreciation—receiving your note might just be the best thing that happens to them

that particular day. Our thoughtful thank-you notes, therefore, can also be acts of kindness.

You may read this chapter and decide the whole idea of handwritten thank-you notes is too old-fashioned or a waste of time, or maybe you feel you are simply too busy. I understand and respect your perspective. But you may also read this chapter and see the value of the virtue of thankfulness or already make this a regular practice. Maybe you are reflecting right now on the written thank-you notes you have received in the past and the positive impressions they made on you. Maybe you are a little stuck and looking for a competitive edge to grow your career. Perhaps you are a job seeker looking to distance yourself from the competition chasing the opportunities you are interested in. Hopefully, you see the best reason of all to send more thoughtful handwritten notes: it is warmer, more personal, more meaningful, and clearly more memorable than the email or texted thank-you messages that have been your primary go-to practice up until now.

One more thing: At the end of his section in Tim Ferriss's highly acclaimed book *Tools of Titans*, author and leadership/marketing guru Seth Godin was asked, "Any final words of advice?" He says, "Send someone a thank-you note tomorrow."

Seth Godin could have left us with *anything*, but he chose this simple call to action focused on thankfulness to thoughtfully end his chapter. Godin is right, and I strongly encourage you to give it a try.

Send one handwritten thank you note this week to someone who fits the example checklist I shared or for some other

THANKFULNESS

reason you deem worthy. Reflect on how it made you feel. Consider making this a practice at least four times a month going forward. You will be glad you did!

CHAPTER 28

Thoughtfulness

Five Traits of a Thoughtful Leader

∽

Thoughtfulness is the intersection of deep reflection and broad concern for others.
ADAM GRANT

My 2024 book, *Becoming a More Thoughtful Leader*, was never intended to be the defining gold standard for how leaders can be the masters of thoughtfulness in their daily work. It's not a novel that tells a story filled with heroes and heroines, and it's not the last book you will ever need to read about leadership. This book was simply written through my passion for reflection and the virtue of thoughtfulness in a way I hope will inspire the same passion in you. It challenges you from the very beginning to thoughtfully invest in yourself and also in those around you. *It was written to be a catalyst for pursuing a deeper journey as a thoughtful leader, not the book you read at the end of the journey.*

PRACTICAL VIRTUE

I suspect you are already a good leader at this moment in time—or you are on the road to becoming one. But have you considered the merits of thoughtful leadership? In the broad spectrum of leadership, *thoughtful* leaders stand out like beacons of self-awareness, empathy, compassion, and wisdom. They not only lead their troops in the daily battles of the work world, but make sure their team members and colleagues are seen, heard, valued, and invested in. They actively practice *Ti voglio bene* (tee vo-lyo beh-ne), which is Italian for "I want your good."

What Are Some Traits of a Thoughtful Leader?

1. **They practice *self-reflection* and value *candid feedback*.** Thoughtful leaders are willing to look in the mirror, carefully consider their past actions and behaviors, and are always willing to learn and grow. They seek candid feedback from team members, peers, and other work colleagues without defensiveness and are willing to make necessary changes.
2. **They are great at *active listening*.** They don't just wait for their turn to speak, but are sincerely interested in what you have to say. They ask great follow up questions and follow up on what they have heard. They make it safe to be open and transparent.
3. **They are *empathetic* and *caring*.** They embody Ti voglio bene thinking, care about others, and always strive to seek their good. They can listen without judgment and seek to understand the other person's perspective, emotions, concerns, and needs.

4. **They enthusiastically embrace the roles of *coach*, *mentor*, and *guide*.** The second of the two challenges I alluded to in the first paragraph was to invest in others. Thoughtful leaders are consistently willing, and even eager, to help those around them grow. They are seeking to both learn and grow themselves and pass along these learnings to their colleagues. They are also willing to be vulnerable and share their own struggles and failures as teachable moments.
5. **They *"walk the talk."*** Thoughtful leaders lead by example. They are authentic and truly believe in what they are sharing with others and asking them to do. Their leadership consistently embodies the behaviors, values, and pursuit of excellence they wish to see from their team members and colleagues.

It is somewhat easy to be a *thought leader* . . . loosely defined as being an expert at something. It is more of a challenge to embrace the virtue of thoughtfulness and care not only for your own development but also for your teammates' development. Further developing the traits above and embracing the learnings from *Practical Virtue* will absolutely help you on the path to being a more thoughtful leader, now and in the future.

I would like to share one more insight with you. As you have likely gleaned from my past writings, I have a great fondness for walking. Much of my writing over the years (and certainly this new book) began with deep thinking that likely had its origin on the walking trails near my home or during family vacations. I believe this practice has activated and enhanced my own practice of the virtue of thoughtfulness and helped me grow in countess other ways. I would like to introduce you to one of my favorite phrases: *solvitur ambulando*, which is Latin for "solved by walking."

The concept goes back to the ancient Greeks philosophizing over the certainty of motion. Thousands of years ago, the philosopher Zeno posed the problem of whether or not motion was real, and his colleague Diogenes got up and walked out of the room. Offended by Diogenes' rude exit, Zeno asked what he was doing, and Diogenes responded by saying he had just proved that motion was real—"solved by walking." Centuries later, St. Augustine of Hippo coined the expression into its Latin phrasing, inferring that theological issues of the heart, soul, and mind are better "solved by walking" instead of just talking about them.

I love to indulge my great passion for taking long walks every day. I do it for exercise, to disconnect from technology/media, clear my head, reflect, and pray. There are many other challenges for which walking is a helpful part of the solution. In our culture of overwork, burnout, and high stress, we're over-connected and distracted from most things that are truly important in our lives. So how do we tap into our creativity, deeper thinking, capacity for wonder, well-being, and ability to carefully consider how to better engage with and help our fellow humans? I have identified walking as a fundamental catalyst for my own pursuit of greater thoughtfulness, and I hope you have something equally helpful in your own life. If you are seeking ideas to jump-start greater thoughtfulness in your own life, I hope you consider the wisdom of *solvitur ambulando* as a possible answer.

As you work on growing your career, I encourage you to take up the challenge of becoming a more thoughtful leader. More intentionally invest in yourself and those around you. Embrace the clarity of author Adam Grant's quote: "Thoughtfulness is the intersection of deep reflection and broad concern for others." The world needs more leaders like this, and I hope you will get started today.

How can you incorporate the behavior traits of thoughtful leaders into your own practice of the virtue of thoughtfulness? Ask your mentor, boss, or teammates to hold you accountable for demonstrating these new approaches and discuss your progress with them.

CHAPTER 29

Vulnerability

Turning Our Vulnerabilities into Something Positive

A leader, first and foremost, is human. Only when we have the strength to show our vulnerability can we truly lead.
SIMON SINEK

If you are reading this chapter, you are human. You are imperfect, just like me and everyone else you know. I hope you will embrace the obvious truth of this but also recognize that most of us are fearful of letting people see our flaws and imperfections—even though we know (and everyone else knows) we have them. *Why is it so difficult to be vulnerable?*

A few clear obstacles to practice the virtue of vulnerability include fear of being judged, concern our vulnerability will be used against us, and not having the right words to use when sharing our vulnerability. We may also incorrectly assume that being vulnerable usually involves the sharing of deeply personal and emotional areas of our lives, instead of recognizing that asking for help, saying we don't know the answer, or *owning a mistake* are also appropriate forms of vulnerability. Perhaps we should consider viewing vulnerabilities as existing on a spectrum from one to one hundred, with more comfortable forms of vulnerability existing near the lower end and more uncomfortable manifestations living near the higher end.

As I reflected on this topic, I came to the realization that the people I am closest to and most admire are all exceptional at practicing the vulture of vulnerability. These individuals are relatable, accessible, and trustworthy. Most of my best relationships exist within this special group. They routinely transform what many may see as their liabilities and challenges into positive strengths that inspire, motivate, and help others. How do they do it? What sets them apart?

Here are five helpful approaches for turning vulnerabilities into strengths:

1. **Use discernment and good judgment.** The appropriate sharing of vulnerability is guided by the use of discernment and good judgment. Always read the room, know your audience, and consider the timing of your words. Be mindful to not overshare. Sharing should always be considered a good thing, but sometimes we need to get to know someone over time before sharing really personal things, and sometimes it's more appropriate to consider sharing one on one instead of with a group. Pick your moments and audience well.
2. **It's critical for relationship building.** Do you have any great relationships where some level of sharing

VULNERABILITY

vulnerabilities does not exist? Likely not. We should all be motivated to build thriving relationships inside and outside of work; the mutual sharing of weaknesses, flaws, and challenges actually draws us to other people. Our vulnerability invites others to be vulnerable. "Friendship is born at that moment when one person says to another: 'What! You too? I thought I was the only one'" (C. S. Lewis).

3. **Tell inspiring stories.** The stories that inspire me most are not always about triumphs and successes but about overcoming struggle, dealing with adversity, or even lessons learned from failure. I often write about my oldest son who has autism. I share his story because I am very proud of how he navigates the difficulties of everyday life and inspires everyone who knows him. Sometimes our toughest challenges, as difficult as they may be to endure, can provide hope and inspiration for others if we are willing to share.

4. **Seek teachable moments.** The best leaders I know are vulnerable leaders. Why? They consistently seek out teachable moments for their colleagues and harness the power of vulnerability to make those moments memorable. For example, I worked with a coaching client some years ago who was insatiably curious, an exceptional listener, and a strong developer of her people. She always wanted to see how her team was doing, where they needed help, and how they were growing. Her "secret sauce" ingredient to those conversations was her willingness to share moments of struggle and failure

from her own career with the team. She was relatable and believable to those around her as she let them know she understood their issues, and her helpful coaching was often the fruit of her rich experiences.
5. **Humility activates vulnerability.** It is almost impossible to truly be vulnerable without being humble. The humility of admitting we are human and imperfect and acknowledging that we make mistakes activates the practice of vulnerability. "The key to being vulnerable is humility. People who cannot come to terms with the truth about themselves—and truth is the essence of humility—will not be comfortable with vulnerability" (Patrick Lencioni, author and leadership expert).

Sometimes, the practice of vulnerability also requires patience and grace. I was not very vulnerable early in my career, but getting married, having children, growing in my faith, experiencing the challenges of life, and the simple passage of time have helped me grow considerably in this area. I have learned to be patient and give myself grace, just as others have extended these same gifts to me.

From my own experience, I would suggest that our ability to flourish personally and professionally is interlinked with the appropriate practice of the virtue of vulnerability. If you feel that you are not as vulnerable as you could or should be, be patient with yourself and do what works for you. Take a few baby steps. Practice being more vulnerable with people you trust. Ask for help and accountability from a few key people in your life. Let's get started.

VULNERABILITY

On a scale of 1-10, how vulnerable are you at work? What did you learn from this chapter that will help you improve? How will you measure progress and who can help you?

CONCLUSION

On one occasion I asked my father what he thought a good definition of leadership was. He said, "Leadership is communicating to another person their worth and potential so clearly they are inspired to see it in themselves."
STEPHEN R. COVEY, *PRIMARY GREATNESS*

As you come to the end of *Practical Virtue*, I want to remind you of the subtitle of this book: *An Actionable Guide to Help You Become a Leader Worth Following*. Nowhere in this book did I offer a magic solution or an easy five-step process to become a leader worth following. Instead, *Practical Virtue* offers you a compelling learning journey filled with invaluable lessons that, if practiced well, will dramatically and positively impact your life and your career. Reading this book, reflecting carefully on the various virtues that also happen to be essential soft skills for leaders, and integrating these virtues into your daily life will provide the catalyst for you to be a better human being and a leader worth following.

I have a great fondness for simplicity. In this overly complicated world filled with distractions, I strive to be a curator (and occasionally the author) of ideas, concepts, and best practices that help us clarify and get to the heart of solving problems, being better people and developing into leaders worth following. This effort is cathartic as I continually work on my own growth and development. Some years ago, I stumbled upon another author's efforts to embrace simplicity and offer something profound to the world when I read author David Brooks' insightful post, "The Moral Bucket List."

Below is a brief excerpt from the post where he explains the difference between *resume virtue* and *eulogy virtue*:

> It occurred to me that there were two sets of virtues, the résumé virtues and the eulogy virtues. The résumé virtues are the skills you bring to the marketplace. The eulogy virtues are the ones that are talked about at your funeral — whether you were kind, brave, honest or faithful. Were you capable of deep love?
>
> We all know that the eulogy virtues are more important than the résumé ones. But our culture and our educational systems spend more time teaching the skills and strategies you need for career success than the qualities you need to radiate that sort of inner light. Many of us are clearer on how to build an external career than on how to build inner character.
>
> But if you live for external achievement, years pass and the deepest parts of you go unexplored and unstructured. You lack a moral vocabulary. It is easy to slip into a self-satisfied moral mediocrity. You grade yourself on a forgiving curve. You figure as long as you are not obviously hurting anybody and people seem to like you, you must be OK. But you live with an unconscious boredom, separated

CONCLUSION

from the deepest meaning of life and the highest moral joys. Gradually, a humiliating gap opens between your actual self and your desired self, between you and those incandescent souls you sometimes meet.

I love Brooks' eloquent message and the clarifying glimpse it offers into what I hope readers will realize after reading *Practical Virtue*. In the early years of your career, just as it was in mine, you are building a *resumé*. You are working hard to earn your degree, gain helpful experiences, get promoted as quickly as possible and build a name for yourself. This early-career pursuit of resume virtue is understandable and necessary for all of us. But there is something more important that building a resume, as David Brooks points out. At some point, we must realize there is more to life than having a great career, and we need to make the fundamental shift to something that is more substantive and meaningful. We have to focus on acquiring eulogy virtue that, long after we are gone, people will remember us for.

Learning and acquiring the virtues in this book will help you grow in character, develop your leadership skills in critical areas, realize the importance of living a meaningful life where work is not the overwhelming focus, and become leaders others are eager to follow. *Practical Virtue* offers a simple, guided path that takes you on a journey to becoming a better human and a better leader. This is the journey I wish for all of us, and it is never too late to begin.

I hope reading this book was helpful, and I hope you will

practice and share what you have learned with others. Thank you for reading it.

How did this book speak to you? Have you reflected carefully on what you have read and acted on the guidance at the end of each chapter? Would you like to continue the journey and go deeper into the world of virtue? Please check out the Additional Resources page following the Conclusion for additional resources to help you continue to learn and grow.

ADDITIONAL RESOURCES

My hope for you is that Practical Virtue not only helped you learn and grow but also stimulated a deeper interest in the power of living out the virtues in your life. I mentioned in the Introduction that I stood on the shoulders of giants—authors who have greatly influenced my life. This page includes book resources from these authors and others I encourage you to explore.

Jesus Christ	All His teachings in the Gospels
Alexandre Havard	*Created for Greatness*
Dr. Donald DeMarco	*The Heart of Virtue*
Dr. Andrew V. Abela	*Super Habits*
Dr. Peter Kreeft	*Back to Virtue*
Andreas Widmer	*The Pope and the CEO*
David Brooks	*The Road to Character*
Dr. Paul J. Voss	*Merchant Saint*
James L. Nolan	*Doing the Right Thing at Work*
Josef Pieper	*The Four Cardinal Virtues*
Jason M. Craig	*The Traditional Virtues According to St. Thomas Aquinas*
C. S. Lewis	*Virtue and Vice*
Cicero	*On Duties*
Greek Philosophers	Various works of Plato, Aristotle and Socrates
Dr. Tim Elmore	Countless books by this great author and his timeless *Habitudes* series are must-reads for all professionals of any age

ACKNOWLEDGMENTS

I am always grateful for my frequent opportunities to speak with students at various colleges as well as early career professionals through the informal mentoring I do each year. More senior leaders like me have an opportunity and an obligation to share what we know with Gen Z and the generations that follow, invest in their development, and also learn from them. My sincere desire to offer a practical and actionable resource to this amazing group of future leaders was the inspiration for this book.

I am thankful for the opportunity through my professional coaching and consulting work to meet weekly with senior business leaders to understand their expectations of early career professionals and also encourage them to increase their efforts to prepare the emerging generations in the workplace to lead.

I want to thank God first and foremost for the humbling privilege to do work I love every day, and I pray it will be for His honor and glory, not mine. I am always grateful for the loving encouragement of my family, especially my wife. Her love and support allow me to do what I do and that means the world to me.

I am grateful for my friends who offered their support for the book, many of them offering the recommendations you read at the beginning or helpful feedback to ensure the book realized its full potential and has the impact I intended. I particularly want to thank Ray, John, Darin, JT, and Tim for your early candid feedback that helped shape the final version of the book.

Thanks, as always, to my longtime editor Claudia Volkman on what is now our seventh book together. Her expert guidance and passion for excellence are a welcome part of the writing journey, and I am grateful for her help. Thanks also to Karen Daniel for our sixth book cover together—her joyful collaboration and expertise make these books come to life.

I am grateful to Dr. Paul Voss for his Foreword and the wonderful insight he gave into the virtue of magnanimity. This book, if carefully read and acted upon, will activate the noble virtue of magnanimity in your life.

Finally, I want to thank the students and early career professionals who will absorb the virtues in this book and activate them in your lives. You are going to the lead the world one day, and I am excited for that day to come. You inspire me.

This book is for you.

ABOUT THE AUTHOR

Randy Hain is the founder and president of Serviam Partners (ServiamPartners.com) and the co-founder of the Leadership Foundry (MyLeadershipFoundry.com). With a successful thirty-plus-year career in senior leadership roles, corporate talent, and executive search, he is a sought-after executive coach for senior leaders at some of the best-known companies in the United States who are seeking expert guidance on identifying and overcoming obstacles to their success or developing new leadership skills. He is also an expert at onboarding and cultural assimilation for senior leaders as well as helping senior leadership teams improve trust, clarity, collaboration, and candid communication. Randy also offers consulting and coaching for companies, teams, and individual business leaders looking to develop more authentic and effective business relationships both inside and outside their organizations. His deep expertise in business relationships is a true area of differentiation for him and Serviam Partners.

He is an active community leader and serves on the boards of organizations he cares about most. He is a longtime partner of the SEC (Southeastern Conference) Career Tour and presents on career readiness topics to the student-athletes and other leadership topics to leaders from the various SEC schools. As a member of the advisory board for the Brock School of Business at Samford University, Randy frequently presents on relevant business and career topics to the Samford students. He served for fourteen years on the board of Growing Leaders and regularly mentors college seniors and the next generation of business leaders. He is passionate about promoting autism awareness and advocating for adults with autism in the workplace. He is also an active member of St. Peter Chanel Catholic Church. Randy has earned a reputation as a creative business partner and generous thought leader through his books, articles, and speaking engagements.

Randy is the award-winning author of eleven other books, including *Becoming a More Thoughtful Leader, Being Fully Present, Upon Reflection: Helpful Insights and Timeless Lessons for the Busy Professional, Essential Wisdom for Leaders of Every Generation, Something More: The Professional's Pursuit of a Meaningful Life, LANDED! Proven Job Search Strategies for Today's Professional,* and *Special Children, Blessed Fathers: Encouragement for Fathers of Children with Special Needs,* all available on Amazon.

Learn more about Randy Hain's professional work, books, blog posts, and thought leadership at his website, www.ServiamPartners.com, and follow him on LinkedIn.